[illegible]nd the Tomb [illegible]

visit guide

texts by
Anna Villari

SilvanaEditoriale

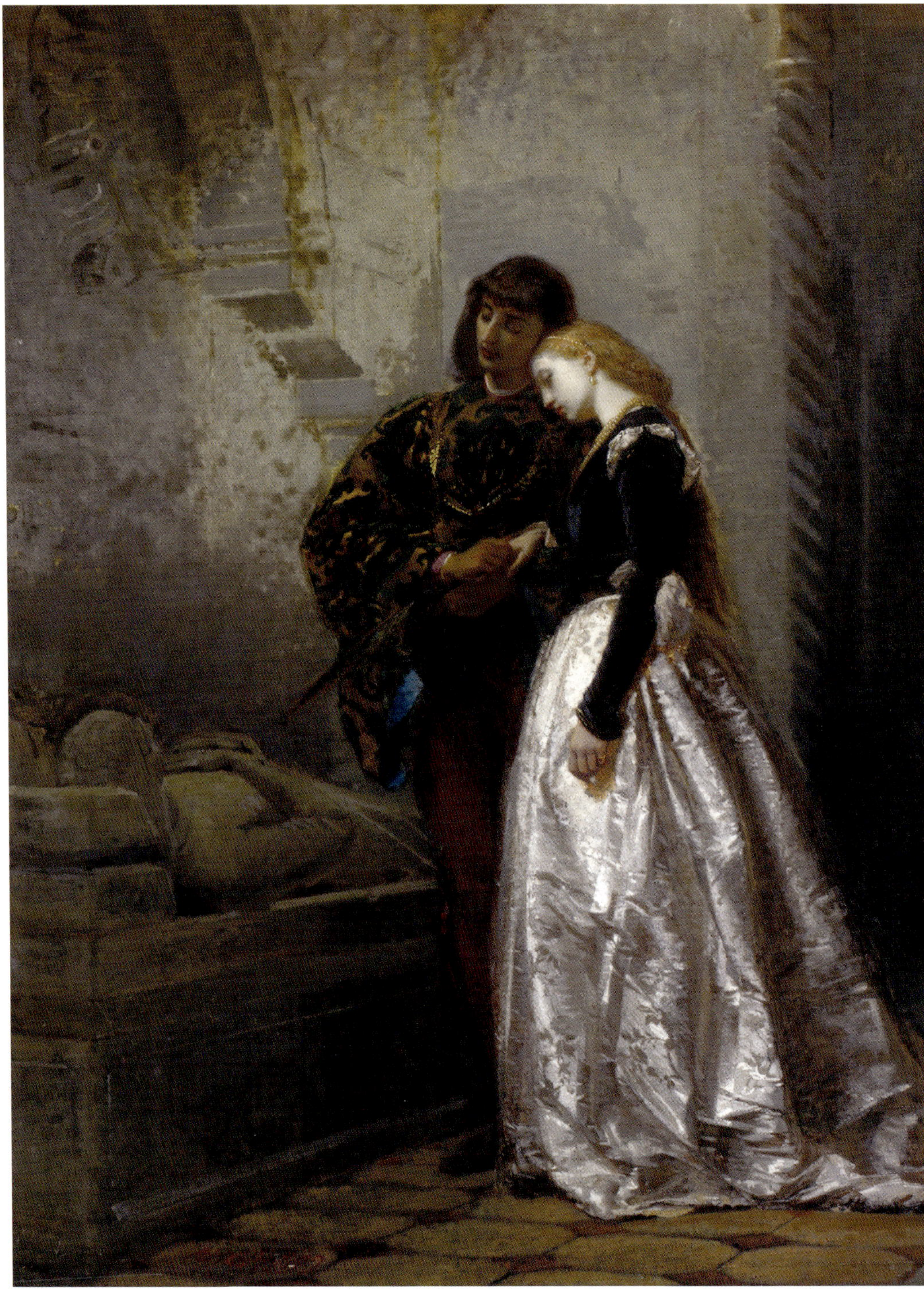

A universal tale of love; a literary subject that flows through the centuries and across all the countries of the world, reaching its apex with William Shakespeare's tragedy Romeo and Juliet; *countless new theatrical and film versions; and finally a vast artistic iconography: these are the underlying themes of the Museum of the House of Juliet, which this guide will be exploring. The guide is not merely an aid for visitors, but a way of complementing and enriching each visit: conjuring again the fond memory of the ritual-like experience of one's pilgrimage to this special site in fair Verona.*
A building complex – bearing the coat of arms with a hat referred to the Dal Cappello family on its internal façade as well as the fireplace in its main hall – the House of Juliet consists in a series of medieval tower houses that underwent substantial changes over time. Located but a few minutes away from the city centre, in an area already part of the Roman grid plan, the House was turned into a museum in the 1930s by the director of the Civic Museums of Verona, Antonio Avena, who sought to fulfil the wish of many of the famous figures who had been visiting the site since the 18th and 19th century, along with Juliet's Tomb in the Franciscan convent of San Francesco al Corso beyond the city walls. Antonio Avena brought to fruition a romantic itinerary across the world of poetry and feelings, bringing together timeless art and the personal experience of each person crossing the threshold into the "dwelling" of Shakespeare's literary heroine.
Because of their immaterial quality, the values at stake here can hardly be threatened by mass tourism – an inevitable occurrence in all the most popular destinations. For the House of Juliet is certainly popular: each year about one million people visit the courtyard and two hundred and thirty million the interior – people of all ages and nationalities whom we warmly welcome, wishing each to feel at home.

Paola Marini
Director of the Art Museums and Monuments of the Municipality of Verona

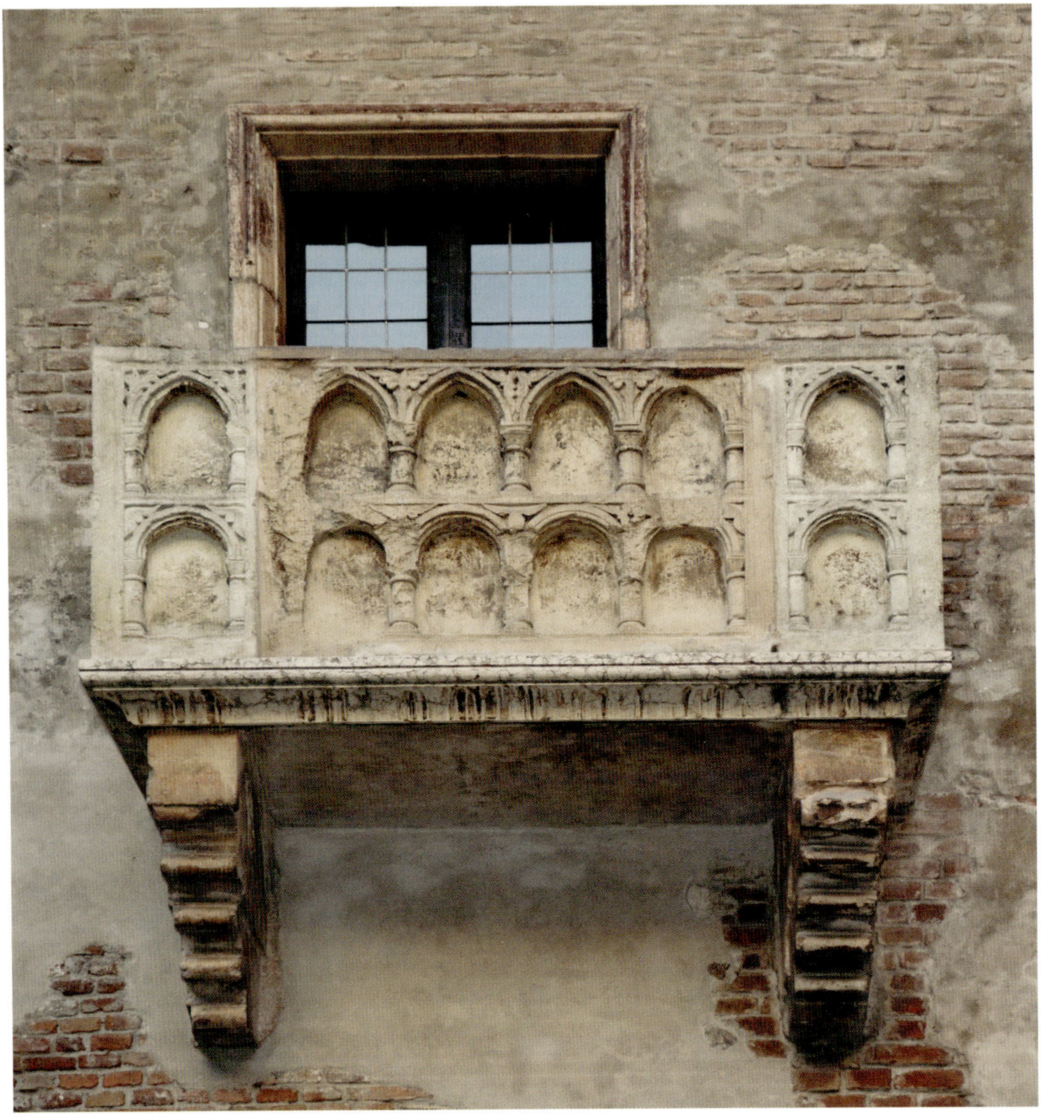

On page 2
Tranquillo Cremona
A Visit to the Tomb of Romeo and Juliet 1861-1862, Milan, Civica Galleria d'Arte Moderna

↑ **The Balcony of the House of Juliet**

The Literary Legend

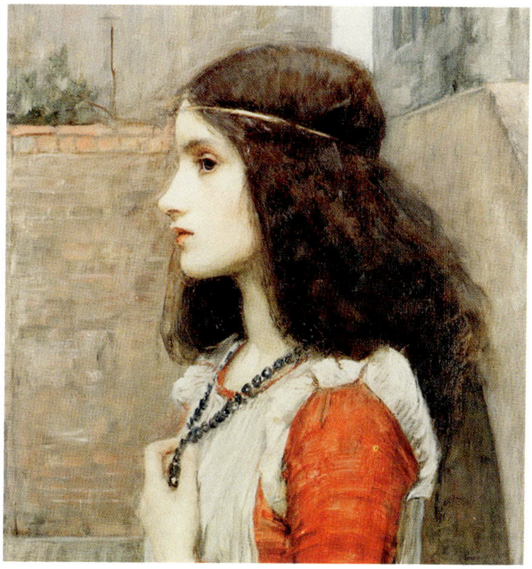

↑ **John William Waterhouse**
Juliet, 1898, detail, private collection

"Two households, both alike in dignity,
In fair Verona, where we lay our scene,
From ancient grudge break to new mutiny,
Where civil blood makes civil hands unclean.
From forth the fatal loins of these two foes
A pair of star-cross'd lovers take their life;
Whole misadventured piteous overthrows
Do with their death bury their parents'strife.
The fearful passage of their death-mark'd love,
And the continuance of their parents'rage,
Which, but their children's end, nought could remove,
Is now the two hours'traffic of our stage."[1]

These words of the chorus in the prologue of William Shakespeare's *Romeo and Juliet* introduce the dramatic tale of the two young lovers. Their story is well known. Short but intense, *Romeo and Juliet* is one of the most famous love plays of all times. The entire action unfolds over five days. Two of the most illustrious families of Verona, the Montagues and Capulets, are sworn enemies. Romeo, a scion of the Montagues, attends a masked ball at the Capulet house. Here he catches a glimpse of beautiful young Juliet Capulet – not yet fourteen – and falls madly in love with her. After the ball, Romeo hides under Juliet's balcony and overhears her vowing her love for him in the night. Romeo shows himself and gets Juliet to agree to a secret marriage. With the help of Friar Laurence, the two young lovers get married the following day. Meanwhile, Romeo's friend Mercutio meets Tybalt, Juliet's cousin. A quarrel ensues in which Tybalt inflicts a deadly wound upon Mercutio. In the happiness of his reciprocated love, Romeo at first seeks to peacefully end the fight, but is then gripped by anger and pain, and ends up killing Tybalt. Banished by the Prince of Verona, the young spouse spends his only night of love with Juliet before seeking refuge in Mantua. Pressed by her father to marry Count Paris, a relative of the Prince, Juliet initially feigns to accept the proposal. On the eve of her marriage, however, with the help of Friar Laurence she drinks a narcotic potion that makes her look dead for forty hours. The friar entrusts a messenger to carry word to Romeo of what has happened, urging him to take Juliet out of the crypt she has been laid in. This message, however, never reaches its destination. Told that Juliet is dead, Romeo lays hands on some powerful poison and then visits the crypt to catch one last glimpse of his beloved. At the tomb, Romeo meets Paris and kills him. He then kisses Juliet and ends his own life. When Juliet gains consciousness, she sees the lifeless body of her lover and pierces her heart with a dagger. Faced with the horror of two young lives destroyed by senseless hatred, the heads of the two families accept mutual reconciliation.

Marked even in its literary language by the play on opposites – for Shakespeare appears to be constantly contrasting different adjectives – the tale of *Romeo and Juliet* represents a tragic intertwining of love and death. The sudden, splendid love between the two young heroes is counterbalanced by a sequence of dramatic deaths. Of the few protagonists of the play, no less than five die a violent death: Mercutio is killed by Tybalt, Tybalt is killed by Romeo, Paris is killed by Romeo, and finally Romeo and Juliet commit suicide. Alongside this manifest and fatal intertwining of love and death, we also find another guiding thread that runs across the whole length of the drama: a sort of oscillation between truth and falsehood, reality and fiction.

This much is suggested by the very title of the

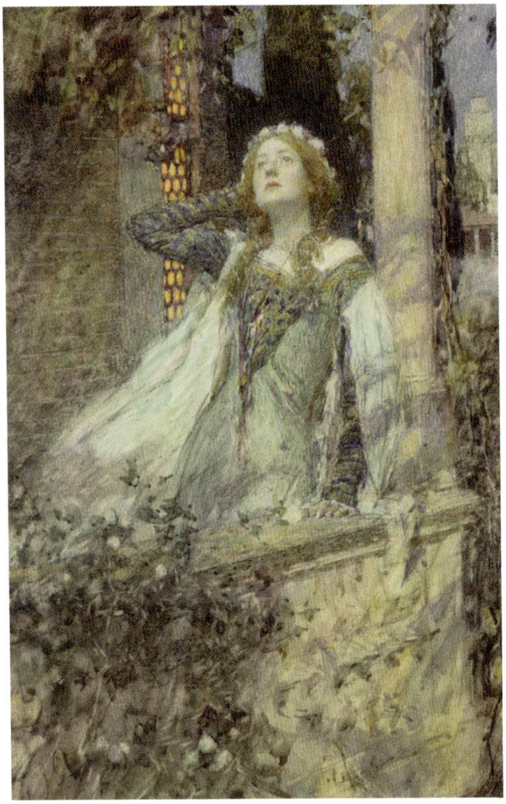

← **William Hatherell**
O Romeo, Romeo, Wherefore Art Thou Romeo?, 1912,
London, Tate Gallery

play, *The Most Excellent and Lamentable Tragedy of Romeo and Juliet*. In point of fact, the work is not a real tragedy at all, and some of its protagonists – such as the saucy nurse – would be more suited to a comedy.

But let us delve further into the plot. When he first makes his appearance, Romeo is gripped by his love for the unapproachable Rosaline. The girl is so unapproachable, in fact, that she never takes to the stage, but is only evoked through Romeo's words:

> "Alas, that love, whose view is muffled still,
> Should, without eyes, see pathways to his will! [...]
> Why, then, O brawling love! O loving hate!
> O any thing, of nothing first create!
> O heavy lightness! serious vanity!
> Mis-shapen chaos of well-seeming forms!
> Feather of lead, bright smoke, cold fire,
> sick health!
> Still-waking sleep, that is not what it is!
> This love feel I, that feel no love in this."[2]

This ardent love, expressed through a tight succession of mutually contradictory terms and adjectives (e.g. "cold fire"), vanishes and is made naught as soon as Romeo meets Juliet. What his genuine love, then, or just a deceptive chimaera? Thinking of Rosaline, Romeo tells his friend Benvolio:

> "Show me a mistress that is passing fair,
> What doth her beauty serve, but as a note
> Where I may read who pass'd that passing fair?
> Farewell: thou canst not teach me to forget."[3]

He later adds:

> "One fairer than my love! the all-seeing sun
> Ne'er saw her match since first the world begun."[4]

Yet within a few hours, Romeo is filled with passionate desire at Juliet's sight:

> "O, she doth teach the torches to burn bright!
> It seems she hangs upon the cheek of night
> Like a rich jewel in an Ethiope's ear;
> Beauty too rich for use, for earth too dear! [...]
> Did my heart love till now? forswear it, sight!
> For I ne'er saw true beauty till this night."[5]

When he makes his way into the Capulet house, Romeo is masked, and so is concealed under a false appearance. The two youths embrace and

↓ **Romeo and Juliet**
Postcard, Photo Archives,
Civic Library Verona

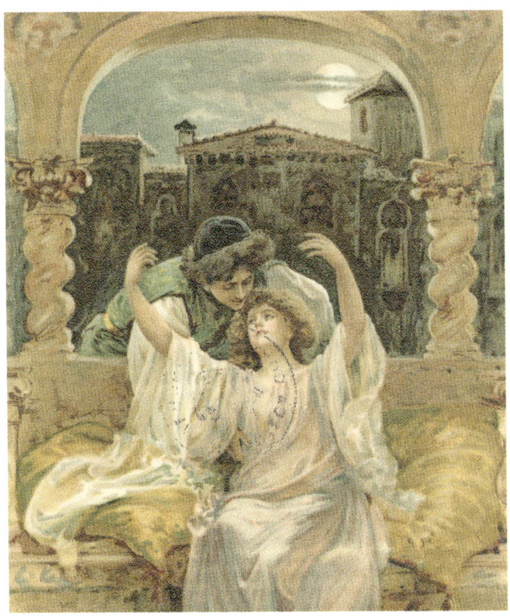

→ **William Hatherell**
Romeo and Juliet, Act V Scene 4, 1912

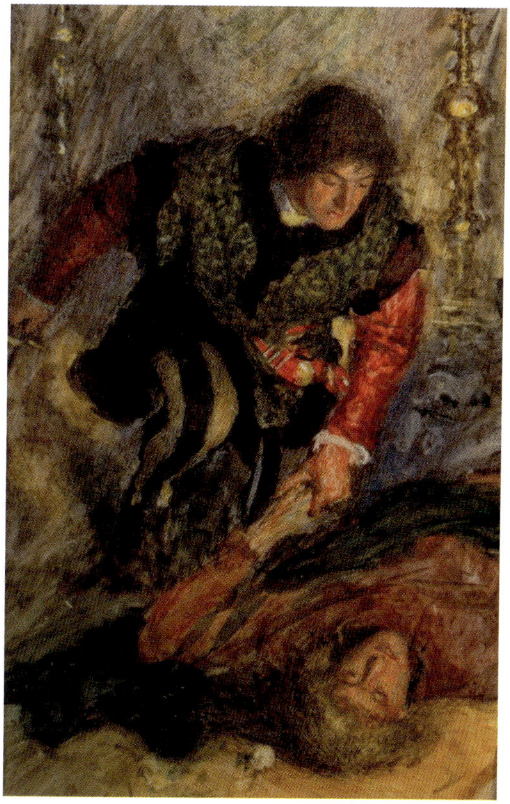

kiss; ignoring each other's identity, they are in the throws of love. But when Juliet learns her lover's name, she breaks out in a heartfelt lament:

"My only love sprung from my only hate!
Too early seen unknown, and known too late!
Prodigious birth of love it is to me,
That I must love a loathed enemy."[6]

Shrouded in "night's cloak" and hence unseen, Romeo later overhears Juliet's love declaration, when the girl thinks herself alone. In this declaration of love – one of the most famous ever – a maiden just past childhood announces she is ready to abandon and renounce her paternal family in order to follow a man she has just met but whom she feels represents the only and greatest purpose of her life.

"O Romeo, Romeo! wherefore art thou Romeo?
Deny thy father and refuse thy name;
Or, if thou wilt not, be but sworn my love,
And I'll no longer be a Capulet."

Juliet then stresses her own lack of interest for enmities among factions and families, something quite inconceivable in an age of seigniories, in which social structures were based precisely on the power of families:

"'Tis but thy name that is my enemy;
Thou art thyself, though not a Montague.
What's Montague? it is nor hand, nor foot,
Nor arm, nor face, nor any other part
Belonging to a man. O, be some other name!
What's in a name? that which we call a rose
By any other name would smell as sweet;
So Romeo would, were he not Romeo call'd,
Retain that dear perfection which he owes
Without that title. Romeo, doff thy name,
And for that name which is no part of thee
Take all myself."[7]

These are the famous words by which Juliet – so mature and brave for her young age – draws a distinction between the underlying identity of a human being and that conferred upon him as a social figure. The old Capulet himself is caught in this web of ambivalence and misunderstandings: he believes his daughter is willing to marry Paris, when she is in fact already married to Romeo.

"Sir Paris, I will make a desperate tender
Of my child's love: I think she will be ruled
In all respects by me; nay, more, I doubt it not."[8]

Carrying on this fatal and never-ending deception, the messenger entrusted with delivering the revealing letter to Romeo is stopped because he is mistakenly suspected of carrying the plague.[9] The unlucky and blameless Paris believes he has won Juliet's heart, whereas she is in love with another man. Thinking she is dead, he cannot but sadly lament her departure:

"Sweet flower, with flowers thy bridal bed I strew,
O woe! thy canopy is dust and stones;
Which with sweet water nightly I will dew,
Or, wanting that, with tears distill'd by moans."[10]

Ultimately, the apparent death of Juliet leads everyone to ruin, so much so that it becomes reality. In a fascinating blurring of literary fiction and real life, this thin line between truth and falsehood also extends to all possible events connected to the story.

The Story

One controversial point concerns the issue of what sources Shakespeare may have drawn upon. His play, written between 1594 and 1595, appears to have been staged for the first time for Queen Elizabeth in the winter of 1595-1596. It was then published in 1597. A second, revised and corrected edition was released in 1599 under the title of *The Most Excellent and Lamentable Tragedie of Romeo and Juliet: Newly corrected, augmented and amended, as it hath bene sundry times publiquely acted, by the Right Honourable the Lord Chamberlaine his seruants*. This edition served as the basis for the final version of 1623. The tale, which sprung from Shakespeare's pen in such a powerfully poetic way, finds certain thematic antecedents in early 16th-century – or even late 15th-century – Italian literature.

A novella entitled *Historia novellamente ritrovata di due nobili amanti con la loro pietosa morte intervenuta già al tempo di Bartolomeo della Scala* (*The Newly Discovered Tale of Two Young Lovers and of Their Pitiful Death at the Time of Bartolomeo della Scala*) had been published in Venice in 1531. Its author, a nobleman from Vicenza named Luigi Da Porto, had passed away two years earlier. The work, which describes the story of Romeo and Juliet in great detail, must have been written no later than in 1524. Still, it appears to have an antecedent in tale XXXIII of Masuccio Salernitano's *Novelliere*, which was published in 1476: the story of *Mariotto and Giannozza*. Da Porto's novella was drawn upon for the drafting of two different versions of *Romeo and Juliet*: one written by Matteo Bandello and the other – a side story within a bigger tale – anonymously published in Venice in 1553 (Gherardo Boldieri was later identified as the author of the latter).

Da Porto's novella was widely read in Italy. For the most part, what circulated abroad was Bandello's version, which Pierre Boisteau translated into French in 1559 with the title of *Histoires tragiques extraites des Oeuvres de Bandel*. This French edition served as the basis, in 1562, for Arthur Brooke's narrative poem *The Tragicall Historye of Romeus and Juliet*. It is this work which would appear to have served as a direct source of inspiration for Shakespeare.

Following this winding course, one might even argue that the story finds its ultimate origins in Ovid's version of the myth of Pyramus and Thisbe, which already contains many of the narrative elements featured in the modern tragedy.[11]

In the course of the centuries, however, the pitiful and gentle tale woven by Shakespeare entered the collective imagination as a historical event. This was particularly the case in the 19th century, when people rediscovered the Middle Ages as a fascinating period marked by passionate loves and political enthusiasms. It is in this century that the debate was first sparked between those upholding the veracity of the play and those denying that it is based on any historical event.

Enquiries on the matter primarily focus on the names of the two rival families, invoking Dante's authority. In that section of the *Purgatory* (VI, 103) which contains an invective on the ills of "enslaved Italy", we find the following *terzina*:

> "Come and see, you who are negligent,
> Montagues and Capulets, Monaldi and Filippeschi:
> One lot already grieving, the other in fear."

As the Monaldi and Filippeschi families really existed and were at the head of two opposing factions in the city of Orvieto – the Monaldi being Guelfs, the Filippeschi Ghibellines – the idea has taken root that the Montagues and Capulets were rival families in Verona.[12] There is no historical record of the existence of any Capulet (Capuleti or Cappelletti) family, whereas documents testify to the existence of a wealthy Montague (Montecchi) family, which was finally expelled from the city in 1269 – prior to the time in which the story is set, the seigniory of Bartolomeo I Della Scala (1301-1304).

Precisely by virtue of these enduring doubts and discrepancies – which may be said to mirror the uncertain and contradictory quality of life itself – the collective imagination has sought to surround the evasive figures of the two young lovers with genuine and indeed tangible places in which to set their tale.

This is the origin of the legend of "the House of Juliet".

The House of Juliet

The Museum of the House of Juliet, in via Cappello 23, is housed within a solid building of Medieval foundation. From possibly as early as the 13th century, this building was the residence of the Dal Cappello family, which lends its name to the street. Over the centuries, the entire complex has undergone much renovation and restoration, as it passed from one owner to another (members of the Failler, Ruga, and De Mori families). Meanwhile, the legend and folk belief emerged that identified the building as Juliet's home. In 1907 the Municipality of Verona decided to purchase at least part of the Medieval complex, namely the block extending along the right wing of the courtyard, and three floors on the side overlooking Via Cappello. Up until the late 17th century, this tall and narrow façade was surmounted by a watchtower. The former presence of this structure is indicative of the defensive and military function of the building. The Cappello family sold the tower to the Rizzardi in 1667.

In the late Medieval period, the building was used

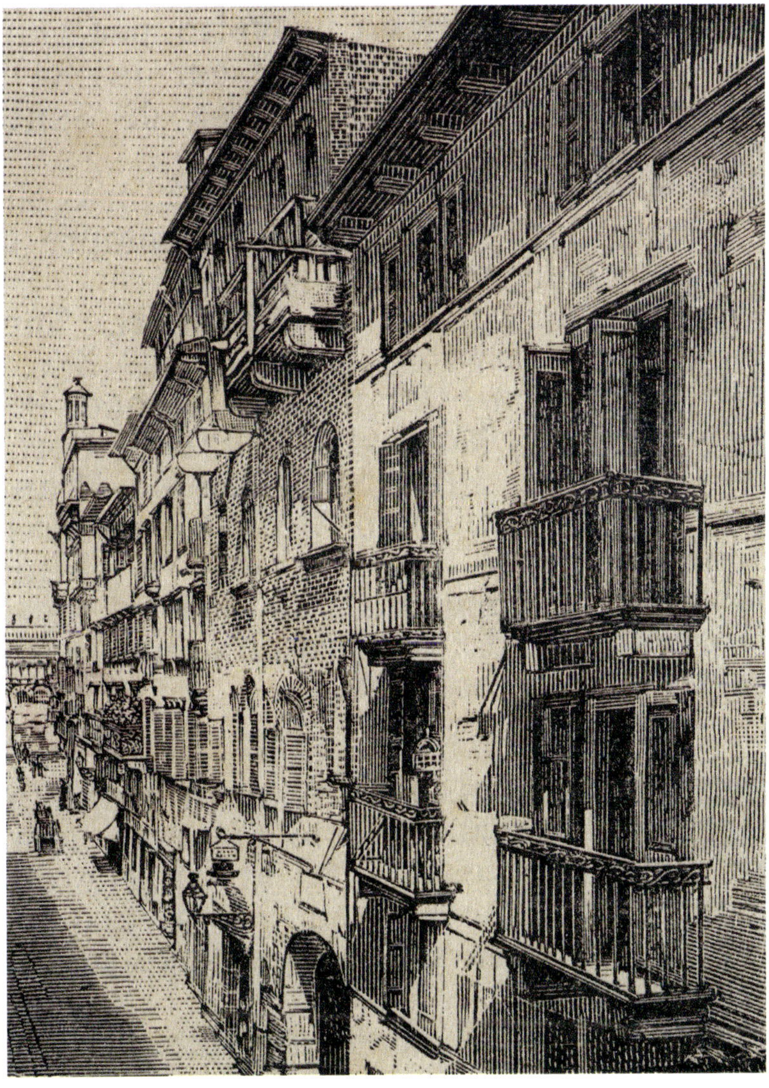

→ **Anonymous**
The House of Juliet, latter half of the 19th century, woodcut, donated by Giovanni Rana

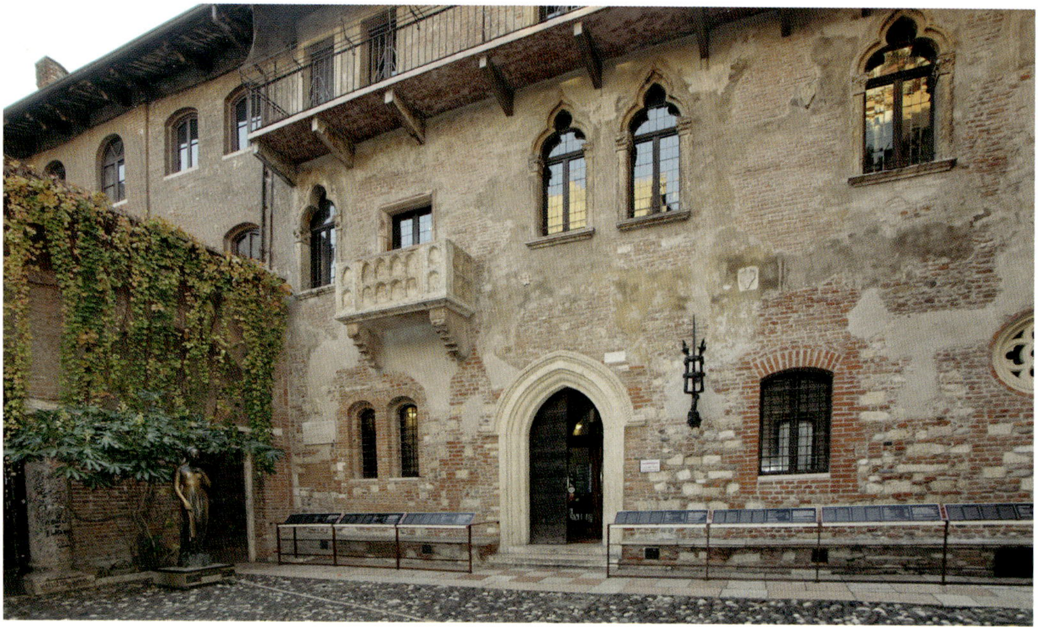

for commercial purposes and as a guest-house for foreign travellers.
When in 1905 the last owner of the building put it up for auction, at the price of 7,500 lira, it was in a complete state of disrepair and abandonment, although its renown as the alleged residence of Shakespeare's heroine was attracting an increasing number of tourists and visitors embarked on a sort of sweet sentimental pilgrimage. In the 19th century – a Romantic period with a "hunger" for passions – Antoine Claude Valéry, an essay-writer and the author of a multi-volume book on travels in Italy, was so moved by the places associated with Juliet that he focused on them in his *Voyages Historiques et Littéraires en Italie pendant les années 1826-28*. Valéry envisaged Verona as the city in which Dante's genius had ideally met that of Shakespeare. In 1828, in the fourth volume of his *Reisebilder*, the German poet Heinrich Heine described "a house, which on account of a hat which is chiselled in stone over the inner door, is supposed to be the palace of the Capulets. It is now a dirty inn for wagoners and coachmen, and has for a sign a red-painted leaden hat, full of holes." Heine, however, concludes by observing that "a poet gladly visits such places, even when he himself laughs at the easy superstition of his heart."
The English novelist Charles Dickens visited the so-called "House of Juliet" in 1846. In his *Pictures from Italy*, he bitterly notes: "Noisy vetturini and muddy market-carts were disputing possession of the yard, which was ankle-deep in dirt, with a brood of splashed and bespattered geese; and there was a grim-visaged dog, viciously panting in a doorway, who would certainly have had Romeo by the leg, the moment he put it over the wall, if he had existed and been at large in those times."
Considering how famous the place was getting, it is easy to imagine what sensation the news of its auction stirred in 1905. *L'Arena*, the newspaper of Verona, launched a campaign to encourage the local Municipality to save the legendary house from the clutches of the "new barbarians". Isolated attempts were made to smooth feathers: scholar Gioacchino Brognoligo, for instance, in the pages of the *Giornale d'Italia*, voiced his amazement at the fact that so much fuss was being made for the house of a girl who had never really existed.
The purchasing of the house by the local Municipality helped tone down the controversy, but did not significantly change the situation. Hence, poet Vittorio Betteloni – the author of a poem in Veronese dialect entitled *Zulieta e Romeo, storia in versi di un poeta popolare* (*Romeo and Juliet, a Tale in Verses by a Folk Poet*) – encouraged the new owners of the building to preserve it "in a more civilized and decent manner than it has been so far, not least for the great benefit of those Anglo-Saxon ladies and misses who with moved reverence visit it, contributing to the tourist industry, which represents a by no means negligible source of income for our country."
The first work undertaken by the municipal administration was simply aimed at improving the décor of the complex. In 1936, the national Ministry of Education authorized the performance of

← **The Courtyard of the House of Juliet**

"consolidation work" for the wing of the building nearest to Via Capello. Three years later, the Technical Office of the Municipality gave the go-ahead for the renovation of the courtyard. Between 1940 and 1942, restoration work was extended to the entire building. The person responsible for this operation at the time was the director of the Civic Museums of Verona, Antonio Avena. It was an essentially "sentimental" and scenographic operation, in line with the attempts made in those years to create specific settings: Romanesque and Gothic elements of various provenance were added, and late 15th-century trefoil windows were inserted.[13] The famous and highly touching balcony was probably a sarcophagus in origin; fitted with the parts that were missing, it was attached to the first floor of the house. The courtyard was demolished and the entire building completely renovated, giving it an artificial neo-Gothic appearance. What has been more carefully preserved is the structure of the building. A deep round arch made of bricks leads into the courtyard, whose right side is occupied by the House of Juliet. Its terracotta façade is marked on the first floor by the white slabs of the famous balcony, with its openwork lancet arches, off-centred to the right. Late 15th-century trefoil windows asymmetrically open up on the façade. The building may be accessed through a Gothic lancet-arch portal. All later work was done on this 20th-century reinvention of the original building. Restoration carried out in 1973 under the guidance of the Director of the Civic Museums, Licisco Magagnato, focused on the renovation of certain interior structures, such as the floors of the building and the stairway leading up to the second floor. The Public Works office of the Municipality of Verona, in collaboration with the city's art museums, then carried out further conservation work on the masonry and pictorial decorations of the building, for the consolidation of its balustrade, and on the polishing of various wooden and marmoreal elements (also on the façade). Following this work, between 1996 and 1997 the rearrangement of the interior of the house was completed with the addition of original 16th and 17th-century furnishings, detached frescoes of the late-Medieval and early-Renaissance Veronese school, as well as a certain number of 19th-century paintings with themes inspired by the story of Romeo and Juliet.

↓ **Nereo Costantini**
Juliet, 1972, Verona,
House of Juliet

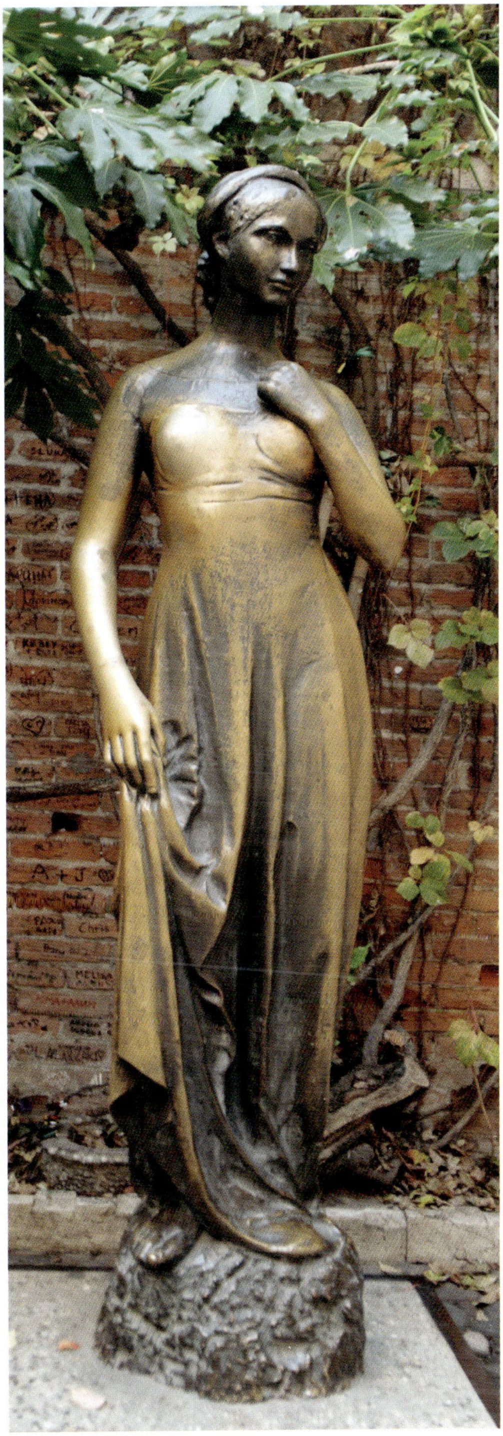

The Museum

A series of artworks on display contribute to the historic and artistic atmosphere of the House of Juliet. On the ground floor of the building we find two 14th-century frescoes, an *Enthroned Madonna with Child* and a *Holy Face*. Both were removed from the Palazzo del Tribunale in Verona in 1875 and may be attributed to the circle of Altichiero da Zevio.

Along with some fine furniture, the first floor houses a series of paintings on Veronese themes or inspired by the tale of the two young lovers. Among these are *La morte di Giulietta e Romeo* (*The Death of Romeo and Juliet*) by Angelo Dall'Oca Bianca – a Veronese painter who was much appreciated in Italy in the late 19th and early 20th century – as well as *Giulietta e Romeo* (*Juliet and Romeo*) by the Emilian artist Gaetano Chierici. On the second floor we find the 16th-century frescoes *Candelabre di fiori e frutta* (*Flower and Fruit Candelabra*) by Bernardino India, which were removed from the façade of Palazzo della Seta al Ponte Nuovo in 1891. Two other frescoes, *Ritratto di signora* (*Por-*

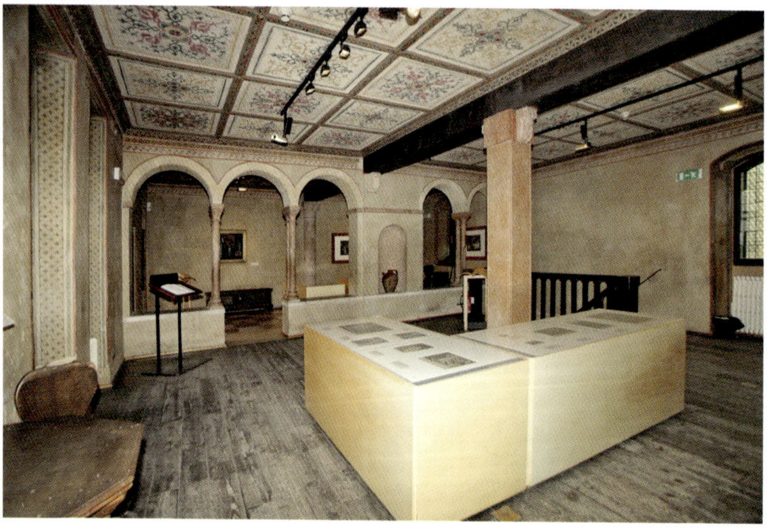

← **House of Juliet**
First floor, Hall of the Balcony

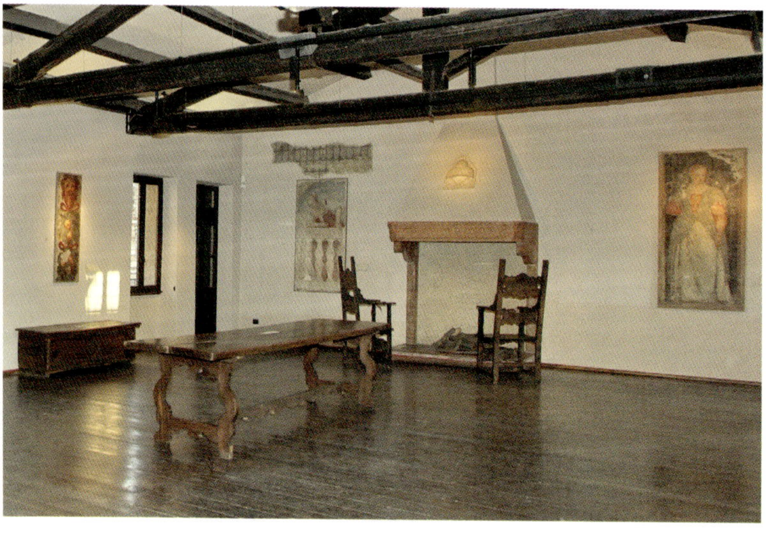

← **House of Juliet**
Second floor, Hall of the Fireplace

↓ **House of Juliet**
Veronese painter of the 14th century, *The Holy Trinity with Saints Christopher, James, and Leonard*

↘ **House of Juliet**
Third floor, Veronese painter of the 14th century, *Enthroned Madonna*, fragment of a 14th-century fresco removed from the Palazzo del Mercato Vecchio in 1895

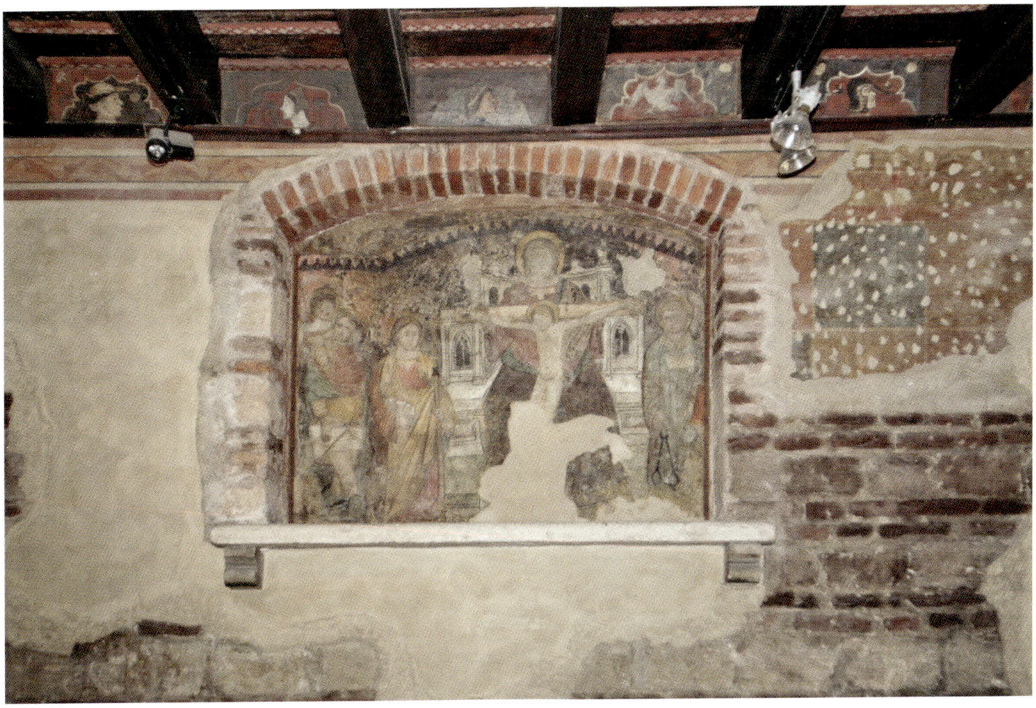

trait of a Lady) and *Donna al balcone* (*Woman at a Balcony*), removed from Palazzo Contarini-Borella in San Marco in 1876, may be attributed to the school of Paolo Veronese. The only place where it is possible to catch a glimpse of the original frescoes of the building is in its main hall. Still visible here is a fragment of a "faux vair" border – that is, a border imitating the ermine fur festoons that were once used as sumptuous decorations in the halls of wealthy homes. Through a covered passageway we reach the three floors overlooking Via Cappello. Here too several elements from other buildings have been inserted, such as the wall consisting of alternate stone and brick ashlars on the left side of one of the rooms. Visible on the upper portion of this wall – which was originally part of the exterior of a 13th-century building – is a fresco showing *The Trinity and Saints*, resting on a bracket. On the intermediate floor is another fresco, again in the Veronese school, attributed to Maestro Cicogna. Depicting an *Enthroned Madonna*, it was taken from Palazzo del Mercato Vecchio in 1895. The wall decorations, featuring geometrical and ornamental motifs, are inspired by

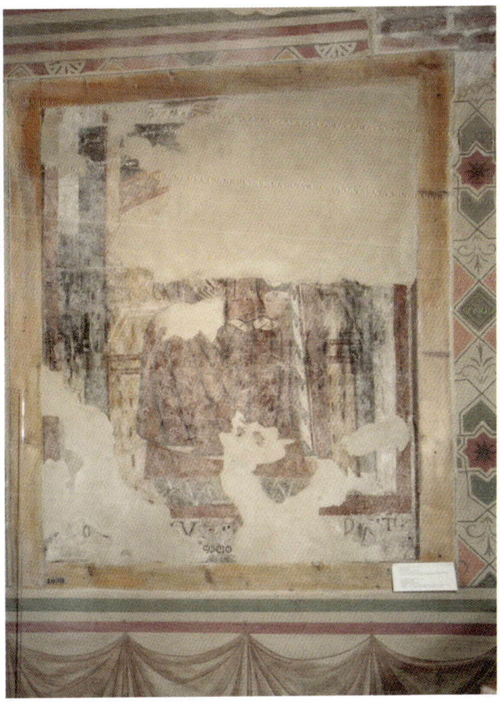

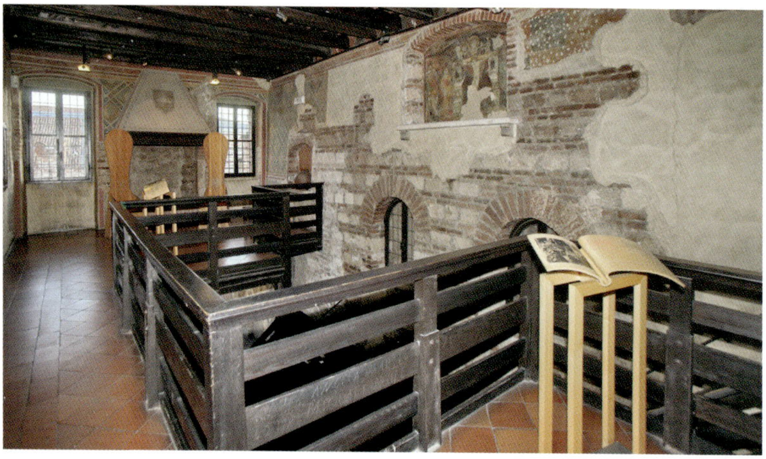

← **House of Juliet**
Third floor

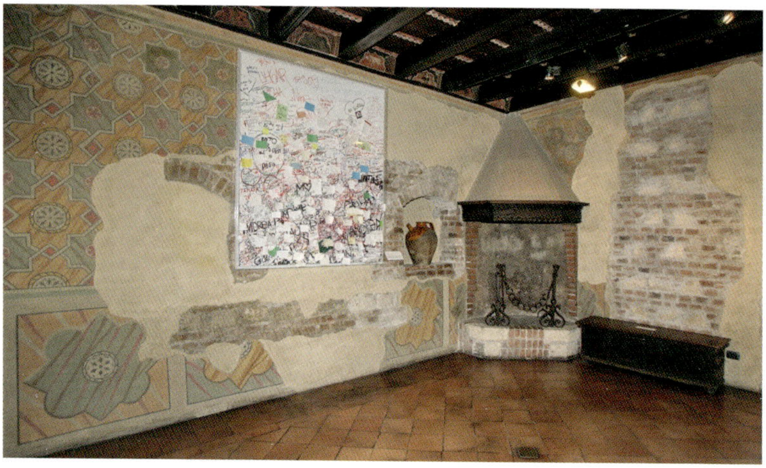

← **House of Juliet**
Room on the third floor with *Love painting* by Mark Quinn, 2009

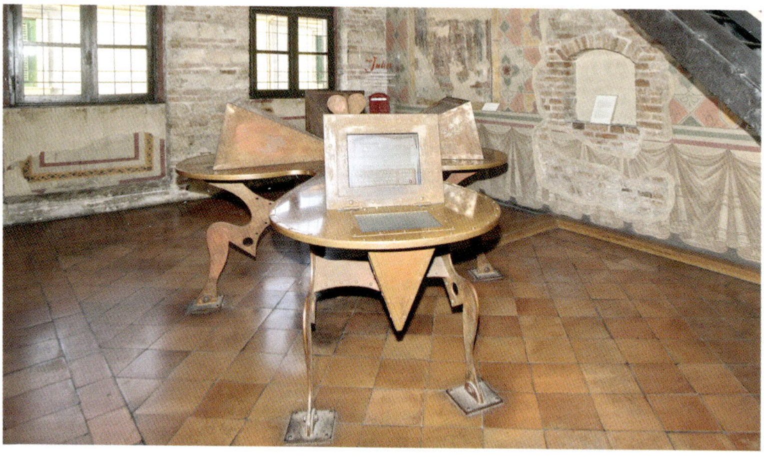

← **House of Juliet**
Room on the third floor
Pucci De Rossi, Juliet's desk, 2003

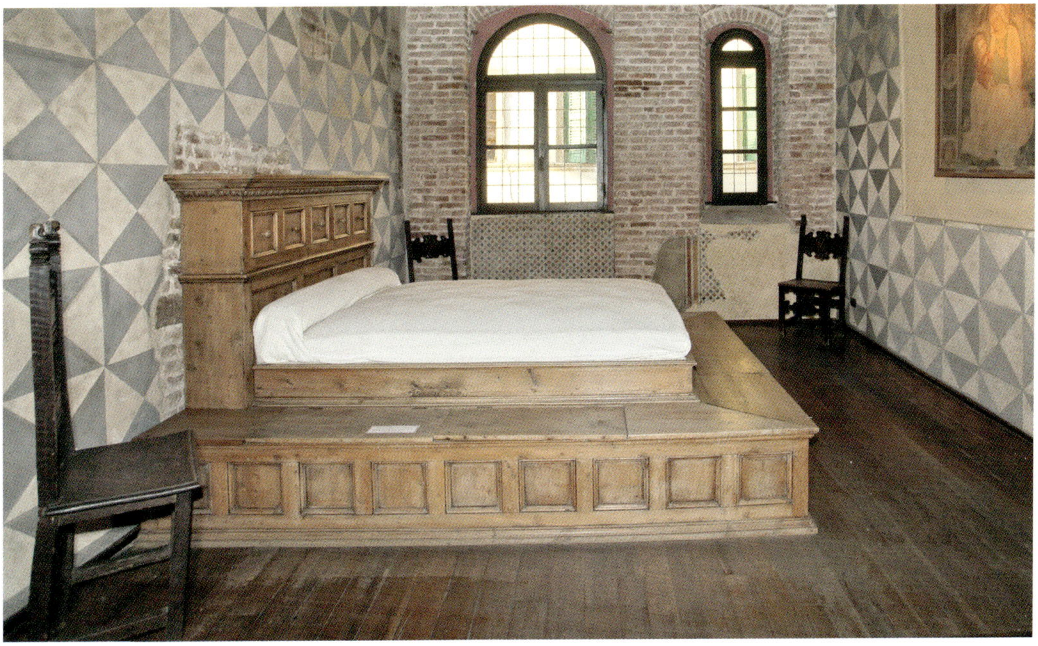

↑ **House of Juliet**
Second floor, bed used on the set of Franco Zeffirelli's 1968 film *Romeo and Juliet*

↙ **House of Juliet**
Second floor, stage costumes used in Franco Zeffirelli's 1968 film *Romeo and Juliet*

models from the age of the Scaligeri (best represented by those in the Castelvecchio), and were recreated from scratch in the 1930s. The last floor

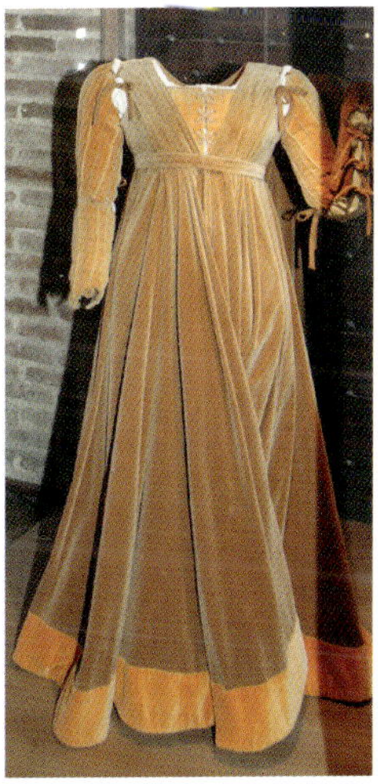

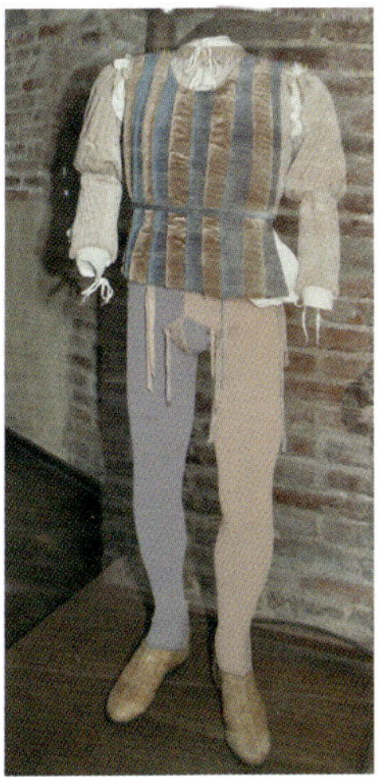

of the wing overlooking Via Cappello houses a collection of domestic ceramic items from Medieval and early-Renaissance Verona; it affords a view of the city walls built by the Scaligeri, as well as of Castel San Pietro.

Since 2002, the Directorate of Civic Museums and Monuments has set up a new exhibit, curated by architect Alberto Erseghe, on the theme of Franco Zeffirelli's famous 1968 film *Romeo and Juliet*. Its centrepiece is "Juliet's bed", which Renzo Mongiardino designed for the film. This picturesque "stage element" was made available by the Imperiale World Services company, which purchased it in 2001 at the auction of the Florentine director's collection. Also featured, along with the bed, are one stage costume for Romeo (played by Leonard Whiting) and one for Juliet (played by Olivia Hussey) – both of which were designed by Danilo Donati, who received an Academy Award – and six sketches signed by Franco Zeffirelli and dated to 1967.

The House of Romeo

↓ **House of Romeo**
Via Arche Scaligere

The House of Juliet has become something of a place of pilgrimage in Verona. In Shakespeare's tragedy, the banished Romeo bids farewell to his beloved city with piercing words:

> "There is no world without Verona walls,
> But purgatory, torture, hell itself.
> Hence-banished is banish'd from the world,
> And world's exile is death."[14]

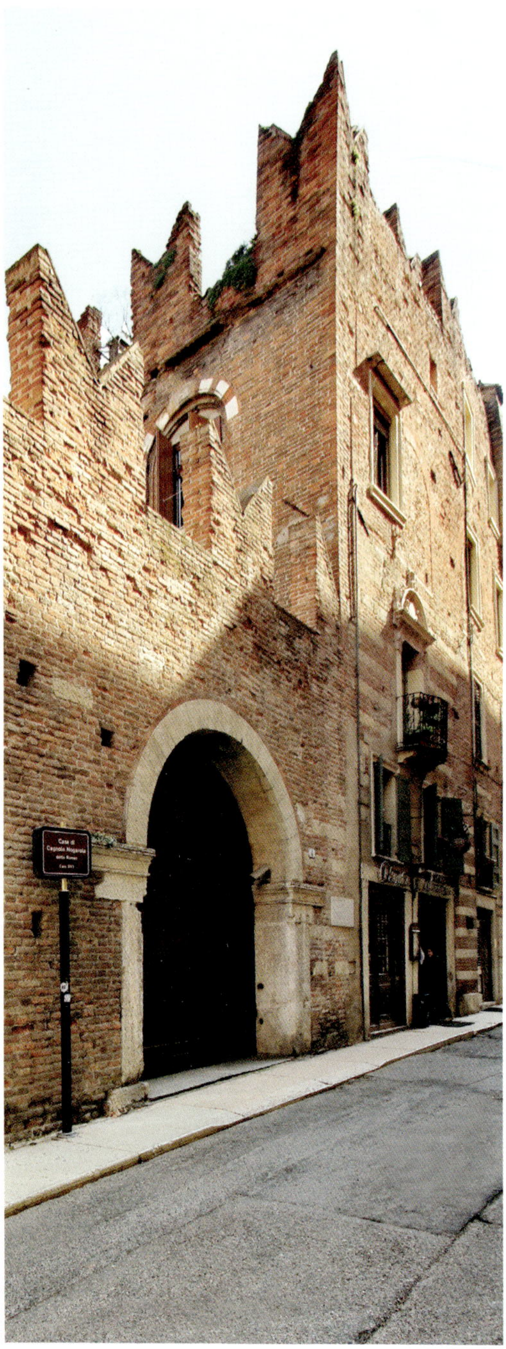

Folk tradition has identified the parental home of Romeo – a character whose soul is so closely connected to "fair Verona" – with a Medieval complex located in Via Arche Scaligere. A 13th-century document refers to the area around Ponte Nuovo as the seat of the Montague family, thus lending support to the widespread rumour that this is where Romeo lived. The building, which has been referred to as the house of the Montagues since the 19th century, is a fine example of Medieval fortified house, or fortalice, and is situated within the oldest circle of walls of the city. Antonio Avena's original project was for the Municipality to purchase the building and turn it into the headquarters of the Superintendency and a Shakespeare museum. Nothing came of it, however, because of opposition from some of the owners and of lack of approval on the part of the Ministry. The complex, therefore, can only be admired from the outside. It presents itself as a compact edifice crowned by merlons, with terracotta masonry marked by the occasional opening – almost an armoured house guarding ancient memories. An elegant Renaissance window of the building, with marble cornices, opens up onto Via delle Arche Scaligere. The side of the house towards Via della Pescheria has instead undergone substantial changes: of the original structure from the age of the Scaligeri only a few arched windows with a terracotta profile survive. A Romanesque portal leads into the courtyard. On one side here stands an open portico – matching the one on the right, which is now closed – with red marble columns decorated with plant motifs and crowned by round arches with a bichrome arched lintel. An imposing stairway connects the courtyard to a stone landing on the main floor, while the floors above are punctuated by Gothic – and Romanesque – style windows.

The Tomb

This itinerary across the sites of Shakespeare's tragic story would not be complete without Juliet's grave. In the play, mention is twice made of this gloomy place. When Juliet is about to drink the potion Friar Laurence has given her, she ponders in horror the idea of being left in such a funeral place:

"How if, when I am laid into the tomb,
I wake before the time that Romeo
Come to redeem me? there's a fearful point!
Shall I not, then, be stifled in the vault,
To whose foul mouth no healthsome air breathes in,
And there die strangled ere my Romeo comes?
Or, if I live, is it not very like,
The horrible conceit of death and night,
Together with the terror of the place,
As in a vault, an ancient receptacle,
Where, for these many hundred years, the bones
Of all my buried ancestors are packed:
[...] where, as they say,
At some hours in the night spirits resort."[15]

Later on in the play, Romeo finds Paris in Juliet's tomb and kills him. Consumed by regret, he then wishes to meet Paris' desire to be buried alongside the girl betrothed to him:

"[...] O, give me thy hand,
One writ with me in sour misfortune's book!
I'll bury thee in a triumphant grave;
A grave? O no! a lantern, slaughter'd youth,
For here lies Juliet, and her beauty makes
This vault a feasting presence full of light."[16]

Juliet's grave has been identified with a red marble sarcophagus in the former convent of San Francesco al Corso (the Tomb may be accessed from Via del Pontiere). Now owned by the Municipality, the complex was erected in c. 1230 and originally included the church of San Francesco and the convent of the Conventual Friars Minor; from the late 13th century it housed other monastic orders.
The tradition identifying this as the place of the two lovers' burial may be traced back to the 16th century. Scholar Girolamo Dalla Corte – the nephew of Gherardo Boldieri, the author of the poem *Clizia* – was the first to mention the grave in the convent of San Francesco ("which I have seen on many occasions"). He states that it was

→ **Tomb of Juliet**
Postcard, Photo Archives, Civic Library Verona

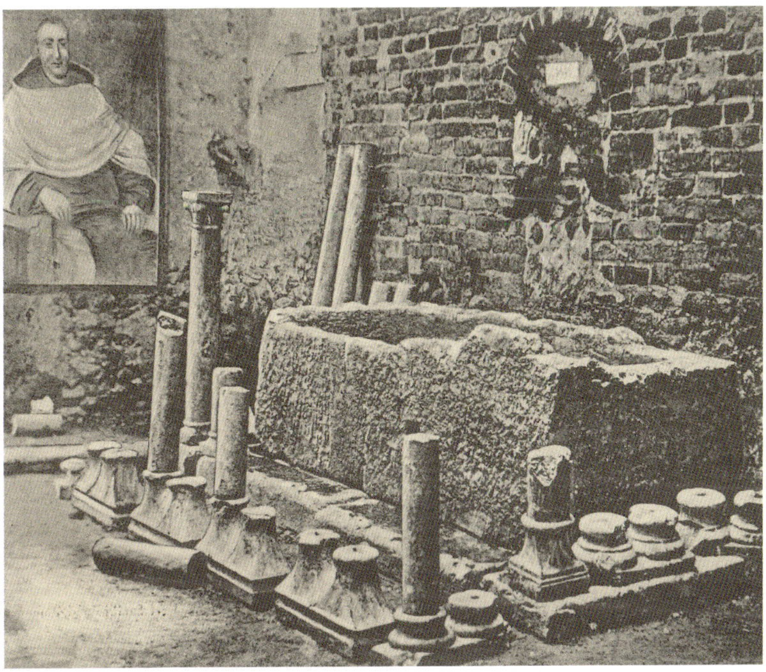

↓ **Frescoes Museum Giovanni Battista Cavalcaselle at Juliet's Tomb**

Sala Guarienti, Paolo Farinati, *Allegorical and mythological scenes*, fresco

↓ **The Garden by Juliet's Tomb**

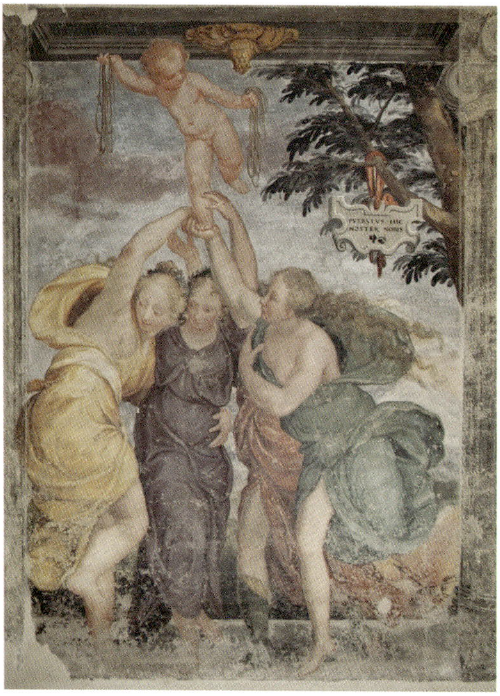

formerly embedded in a wall opposite the convent.[17] The sources indeed confirm that the sarcophagus was removed from the wall as early as in 1548 by orders of the ecclesiastical authorities – who may have disapproved of the veneration that it was starting to attract – and was turned into a water-trough.

In the early decades of the 19th century, the tomb became the object of a sort of vaguely superstitious worship, to the point that visitors often removed fragments of it, as if these were sacred relics. In 1820 the Veronese historian Giambattista Da Persico described the grave in the following terms: "It is left to go to ruin, for day after day it dwindles, as people remove portions of it to make jewels." Many people took part in this looting, including famous tourists such as Marie Louise of Habsburg-Lorraine, Duchess of Parma, who in 1822 collected various fragments from which she made a necklace. The English poet George Byron, while charmed by the secluded melancholy of the place, recalled: "I have brought away a few pieces of the granite, to give to my daughter and my nieces." According to playwright August von Kotzebue, around the years 1815-1820 Archduke John of Austria took the lid of the sarcophagus to Vienna (which is where the writer saw it).

Partitioned and pillaged, by the mid-19th century the tomb already lay in a serious state of disrepair, serving – as Dickens noted – as a sort of "water-

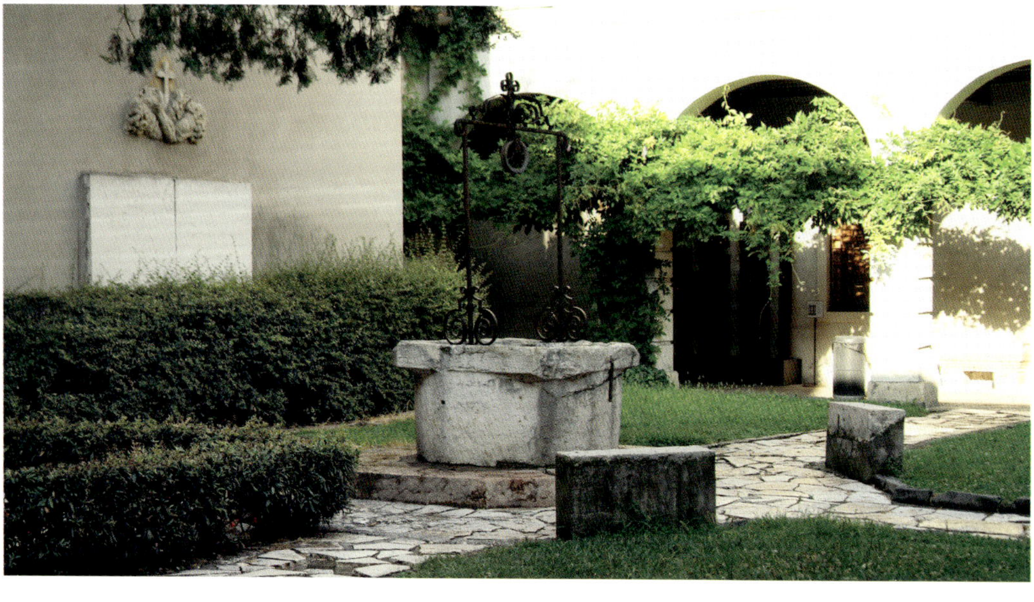

↓ **Tomb of Juliet**
Postcard, Photo Archives,
Civic Library Verona

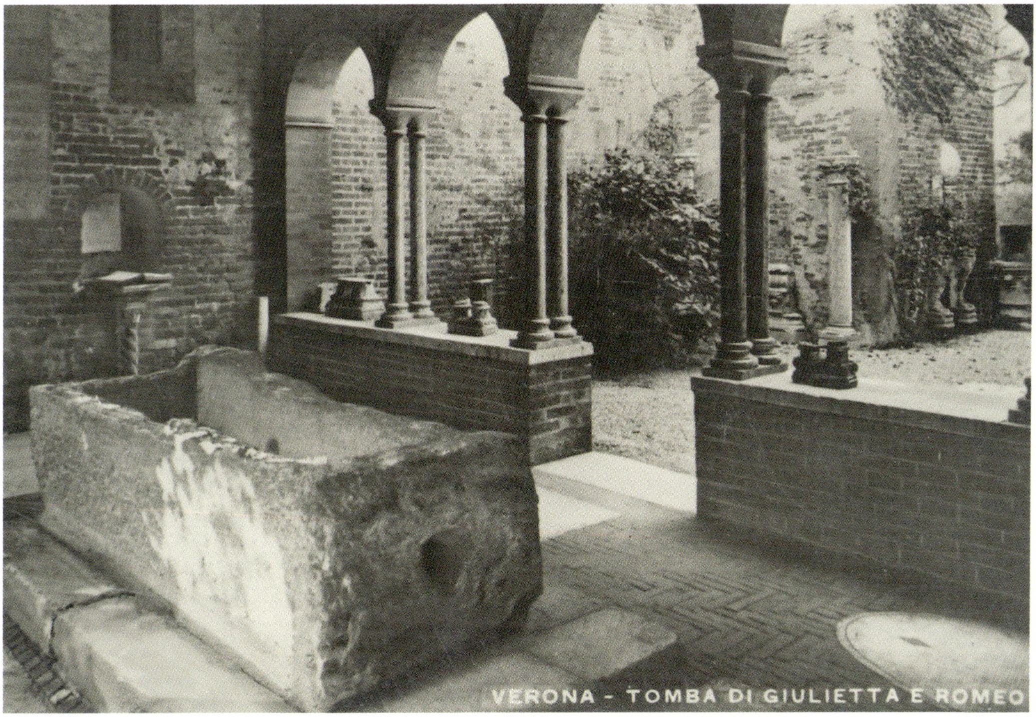

↓ **Tomb of Juliet**
In the museum complex
of San Francesco al Corso

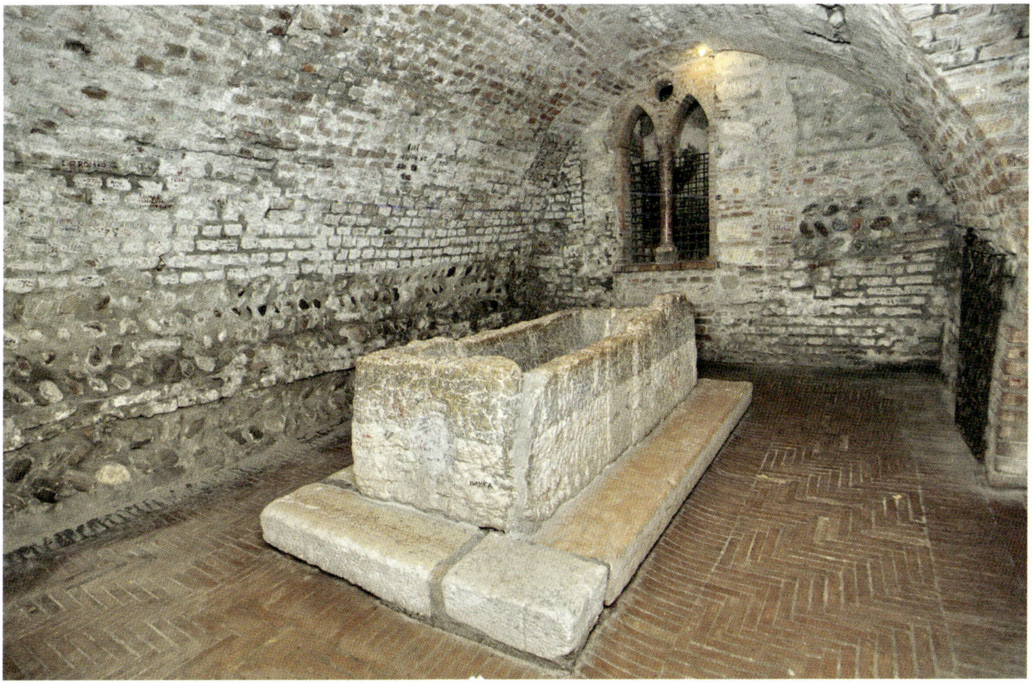

trough". In 1868, the Congregazione di Carità (Charity Congregation), which owned the building at the time, chose to move the sarcophagus to a more fitting location. A kind of small chapel was built from two of the walls of the ancient church that were still standing, with the addition of architectural structures from the cloister of San Francesco. The sarcophagus was fenced off in the late 19th century and in 1910 a marble bust of Shakespeare by sculptor Renato Cattani was added. In 1938 Antonio Avena received permission from the national Ministry of Education to begin renovation work, wherewith the grave was moved to its present location. The bust of Shakespeare that stood in the garden beyond the convent walls was placed under the portico by the entrance leading to the underground area. Via delle Franceschine was opened again, and now a small shaded avenue leads to Via del Pontiere. From here two underground rooms can be accessed, the smaller of which houses the sarcophagus. The western section of the complex was destroyed by bombing in 1944-1945, while the 14th-century bell tower crumbled in 1959, as did part of the cloister in 1978.[18]

The complex was turned into an exhibit site in 1970, when Licisco Magagnato was director of the Civic Museums. In 1973 the Museo degli affreschi (Frescoes Museum) was inaugurated. Named after the great art historian Giovanni Battista Cavalcaselle, it is located on the upper floors of the western wing of the convent, which was rebuilt after it was bombed.

The Museum houses frescoes of different periods from churches, interiors, and especially the façades of ancient buildings in Verona, which used to be known as the *urbs picta* (painted city) on account of the splendid and colourful decorations adorning many of its palaces.

Collected in the Museum are some interesting examples of Veronese painting, such as for instance frescoes from churches, façades and home interiors, many of which are found in the city thanks to the widespread practice in Renaissance times of decorating public palaces. These frescoes were removed in the 19th century to ensure their conservation, particularly following the devastating flood of the Adige river in 1882. On display are some of the oldest paintings in Verona, such as the frescoes from the chapel of the Saints Nazzaro and Celso (11th-12th cent.), large fragments of the fresco decorations from the façade of Palazzo Fiorio della Seta (mid-16th cent.), and other fragments from a hall of Palazzo Guarienti with allegorical themes set within faux architectural structures, which were painted around 1560 by Paolo Farinati (1524-1606). Also to be found in the Museum are some 19th-century sculptures by Veronese artists, such as Innocenzo Fraccaroli (1805-1882) – a pupil of Bertel Thorvaldsen and Pietro Tenerani – and Torquato Della Torre (1827-1855).

In the 1960s restoration work was also carried out on the church of San Francesco, which was converted into a museum in 1987. This now houses paintings in the Veronese school from the 16th to 18th century, including works by Giovan Francesco Caroto (c.1480 - c.1555), Domenico Morone (c. 1440 - *post* 1517), Girolamo Bonsignori (c. 1472-1529), Louis Dorigny (1654-1742), Antonio Balestra (1666-1740).

↗ **G.S. Facius and J.G. Facius**
After J. Opie, *Shakespeare: Juliet's Death*, 1791, etching and dotted etching, donated by Giovanni Rana

→ **P. Simon**
After James Northcote, *Shakespeare: Romeo's Death*, 1792, etching and dotted etching, donated by Giovanni Rana

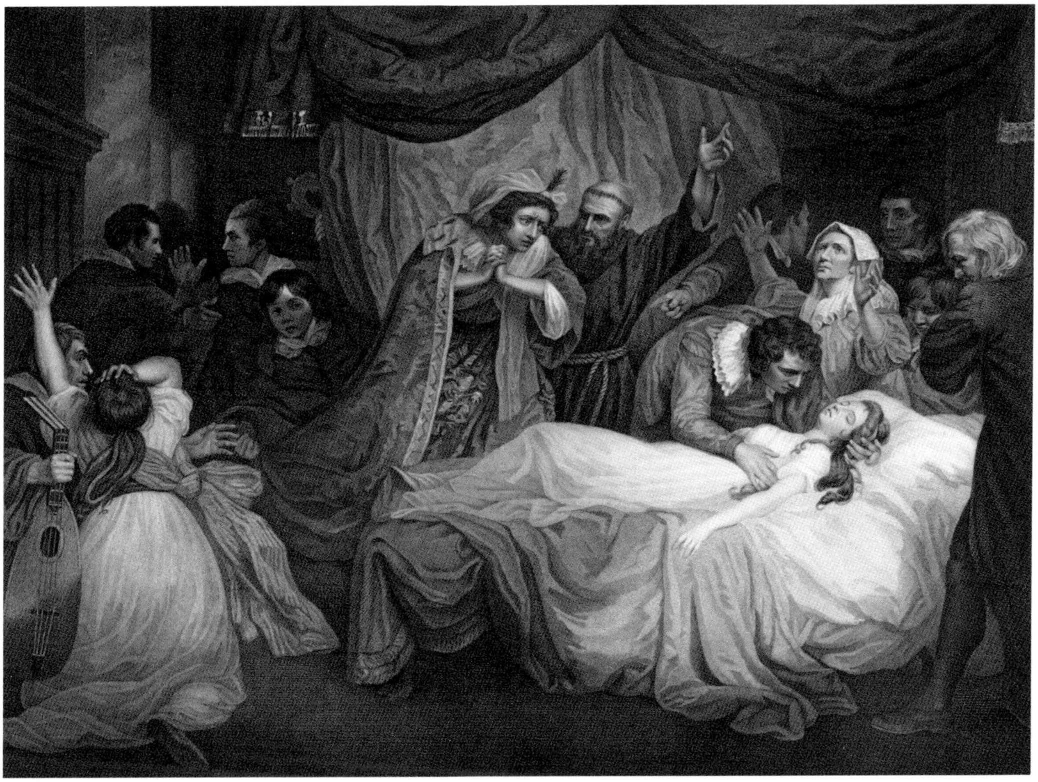

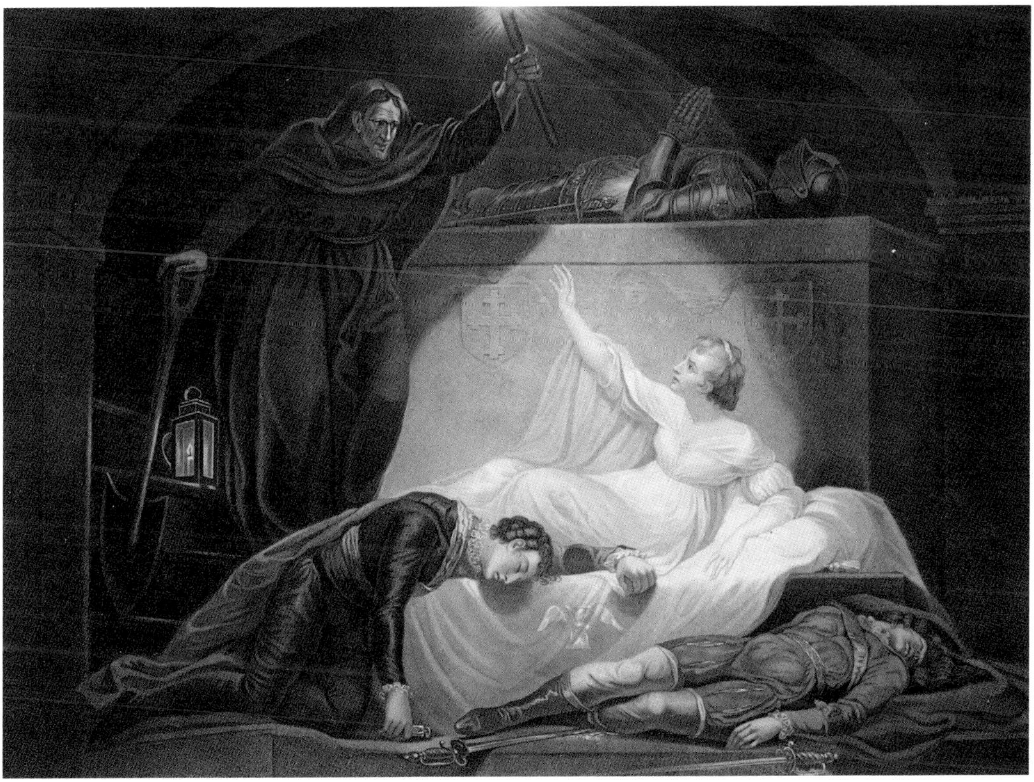

The Legend's Fortune in Figurative Art

↙ **Frank Dicksee**
Romeo and Juliet, 1884,
Southampton City Art Gallery

The graceful literary ghosts of Romeo and Juliet, whose presence can almost be felt in Verona, would have remained incorporeal and evanescent, had painters enchanted by the story not lent them looks, attitudes, fine clothes and a proper setting, as shown for instance by the splendid illustrations made of Da Porto's novella (only a few example of which survive on parchment). The edition of this work published in Milan in 1819 features drawings by the exquisite miniaturist Giambattista Gigola of Brescia (fig. page 26).
As already noted, the entire narrative unfolds over a very short period of time and is marked by a pair of opposites: love and death. These are the two themes that have captured the creative verve of modern artists, both in Italy and abroad: the kiss – or rather one of the very few kisses – exchanged by the couple of unfortunate lovers (either in the evening of their first meeting or on the morning of their parting, after the only night they were fated to spend together), and the theme of death. This death – ever more tragic as it is caused by chance events – is often followed by a mournful yet grand funeral procession, such as that envisaged by the Roman artist Scipione Vannutelli in his 1888 painting *I funerali di Giulietta* (*Juliet's Funerals*) (fig. page 26).
It is particularly the kiss accompanying Romeo's announced departure – "Farewell, farewell! one kiss, and I'll descend"[19] – which has been immortalized. Painters have depicted the encounter between the two lovers in a number of different ways, as if it were a musical score open to subtle variations.
In 1823 Francesco Hayez executed his *L'ultimo bacio dato a Giulietta da Romeo* (*The Last Kiss given to Juliet by Romeo*) (fig. page 23) subject on which recur frequently in the future. The painter was thirty-two at the time: a young man who wished to affirm the sweeping power of love both in his art and in real life. The painting elicited chastisement from art critics such as Ludwig Schörn, who regarded Juliet's visage and appearance as not idealizing enough and too explicitly lascivious. The figure of Juliet is modelled after Hayez's pupil and uninhibited lover Caterina Zucchi. But it is precisely the fresh passion of this young girl – her flesh still bearing traces of the warmth of her bed,

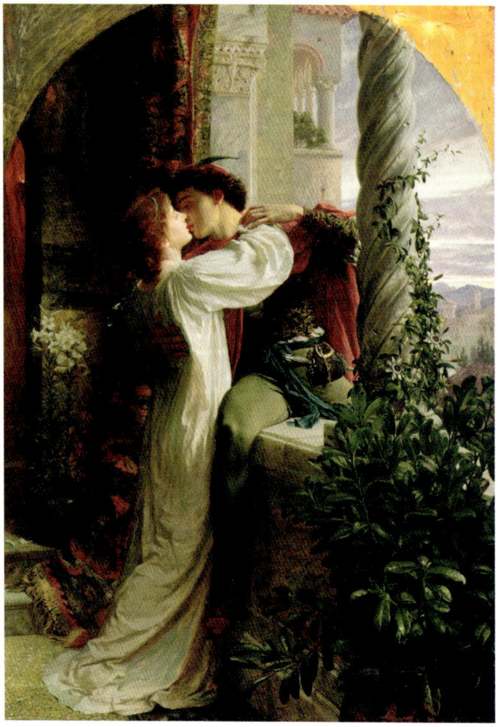

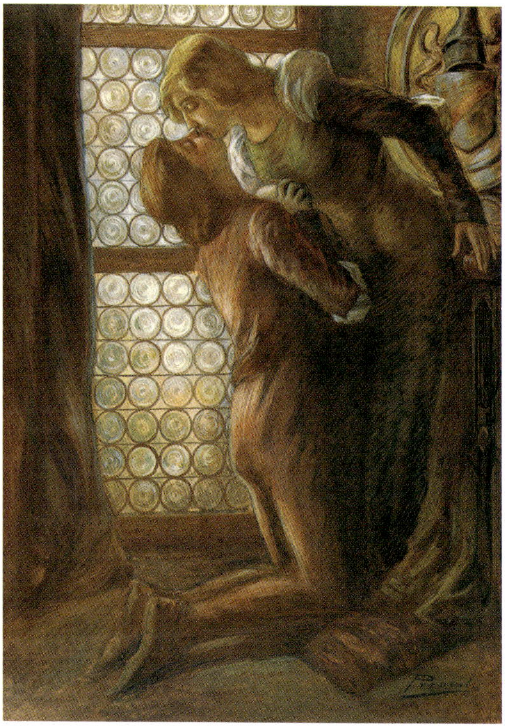

↙ **Richard Dadd**
Sketch for the Passions. Love, 1853, Yale Center for British Art

↘ **Francesco Hayez**
The Last Kiss given to Juliet by Romeo, 1823, Villa Carlotta, Tremezzo (Como)

her soft contour those of the childhood she has just grown out of – that makes her appear so genuine and vibrant in modern eyes. Romeo, whose pose and clothing is more theatrical, in turn acquires a lifelike quality through the possessive yet tender gesture of his open hand, as he grips the maiden's waist and pushes her body against his own. In 1830 Hayez focused on the theme once more with *L'ultimo addio di Giulietta e Romeo* (*The Last Farewell of Romeo and Juliet*). This canvas has gone missing, but a watercolour version in a private collection shows the two lovers suspended in the moment just before their kiss – Juliet's face turned upwards and her eyes closed, as a most elegant Romeo timidly draws towards her.
Various renditions of the tale appeared in Italy and France (including two versions painted by Eugène Delacroix in 1845 and 1851: his *Parting of Romeo and Juliet* – now in a private collection – and *Romeo and Juliet at the Tomb of the Capulets*, which has gone missing). The theme became very popular of course in England, Shakespeare's home country, which in the 19th century was steeped in love for Italy and its history. In his 1870 painting *Romeo and Juliet* (fig. page 25), Ford Madox Brown depicts an exterior scene on a balcony, with Romeo as the main figure. Caught in the foreground and dressed in red, as he is about to cross the balustrade, Romeo suddenly flings himself towards Juliet – her garments loose, her face framed by her curly hair, and her eyes half-closed in the languor of love and pain of separation – passionately seeking to kiss her neck. More chastely idealizing is Frank Dicksee's 1884 *Romeo and Juliet* (fig. page 22). Here the two pale but composed protagonists – Juliet's white dress contrasting with Romeo's red cloak – are surrounded by plants and flowers (including a symbolic passion flower, which creeps up the spiral column of the veranda). The figures are particularly touching because of their young age: they are more like a boy and a girl exchanging their first innocent kiss than Shakespeare's passionate and ill-fated lovers.
Gaetano Previati's 1889 painting *Il bacio* (*The Kiss* – Milan, private collection) is more deeply steeped in the kind of erotic feeling sparked between the two youths at their very first meeting ("If I profane with my unworthiest hand / This holy shrine, the gentle fine is this: / My lips, two blushing pilgrims, ready stand / To smooth that rough touch with a tender kiss").[20]
These nocturnal languors are countered by nocturnal horrors: the sepulchre, death, and the foetid air dreaded by Juliet. Already in 1789, as part of John Boydell's project of commissioning illustrations of Shakespeare's works from different artists, James Northcote painted *A Monument Belonging to the Capulets. Romeo and Paris Dead. Juliet and Friar Lawrence*, which shows Juliet illumined by the light of a torch at the centre of the scene, caught in a gesture of desperate dismay. The same miserable impression is made by a painting executed by Pietro Roi (fig. page 27) – a painter of Purist background – over sixty years later. In this work, marked by dramatic contrasts of colours, a pearly Juliet stands out against the deep black "Spanish" hues of Romeo's body. Even more intensely and sombrely tragic are the two paintings executed at the beginning of the century by Swiss artist Johann Heinrich Füssli, who on several occasions engaged with Shakespearian themes. His *Romeo Stabs Paris at the Bier of Juliet* renders the sombre violence of a dramatic episode

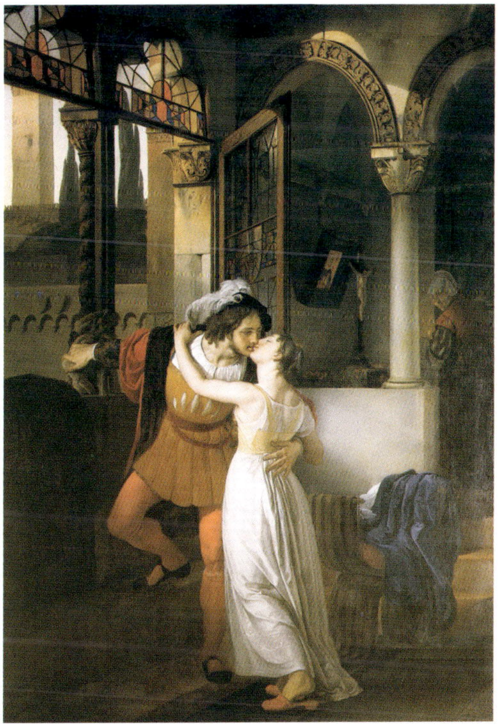

↓ **John Henry Frederick Bacon**
Edith Nesbit, *Romeo and Juliet*, from *Beautiful Stories from Shakespeare* by private collection: Bridgeman Art Library/Alinari Archives (Bacon, John Henry Frederick)

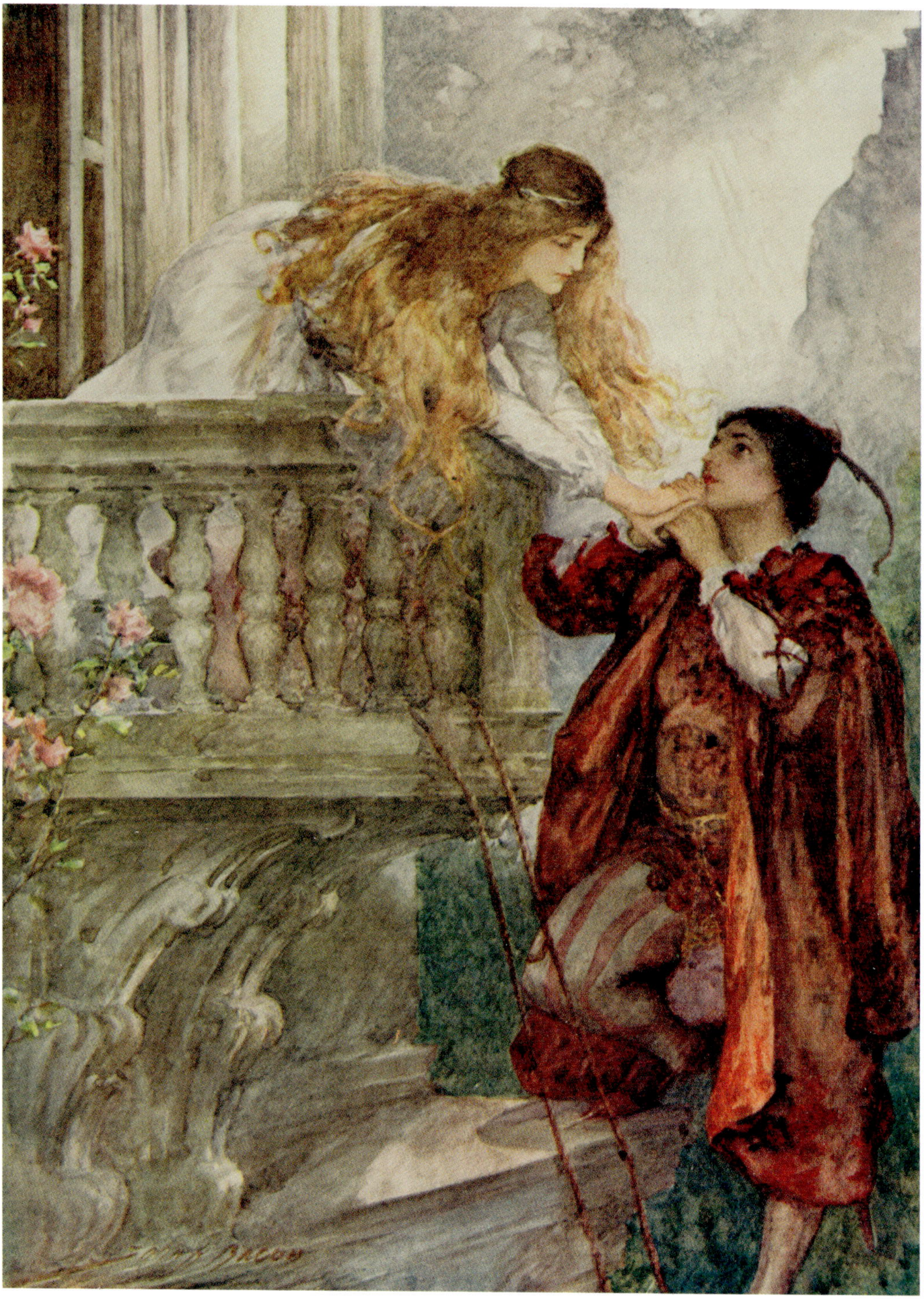

↓ **Ford Madox Brown**
Romeo and Juliet, 1870,
Birmingham Museums
and Art Gallery

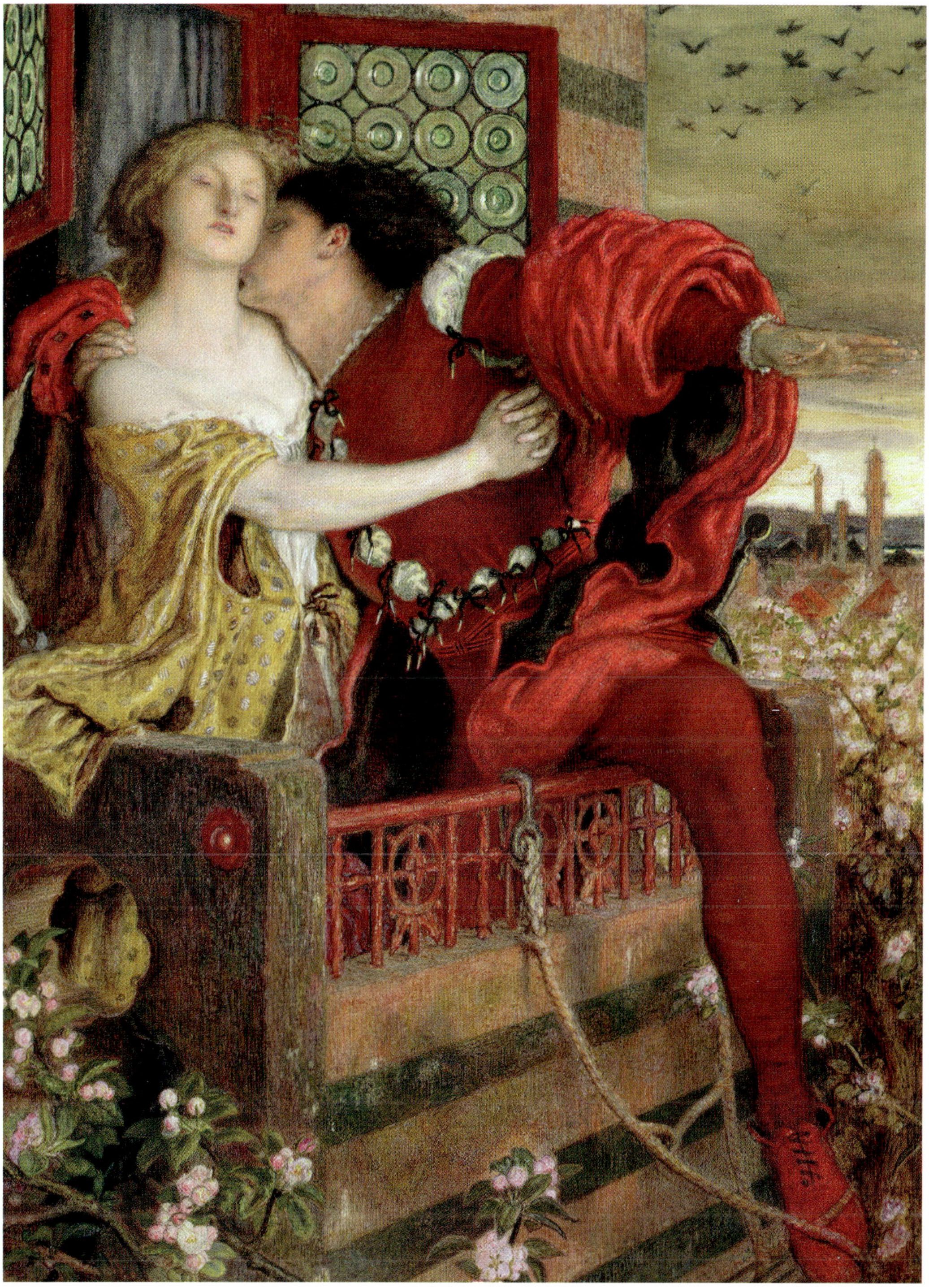

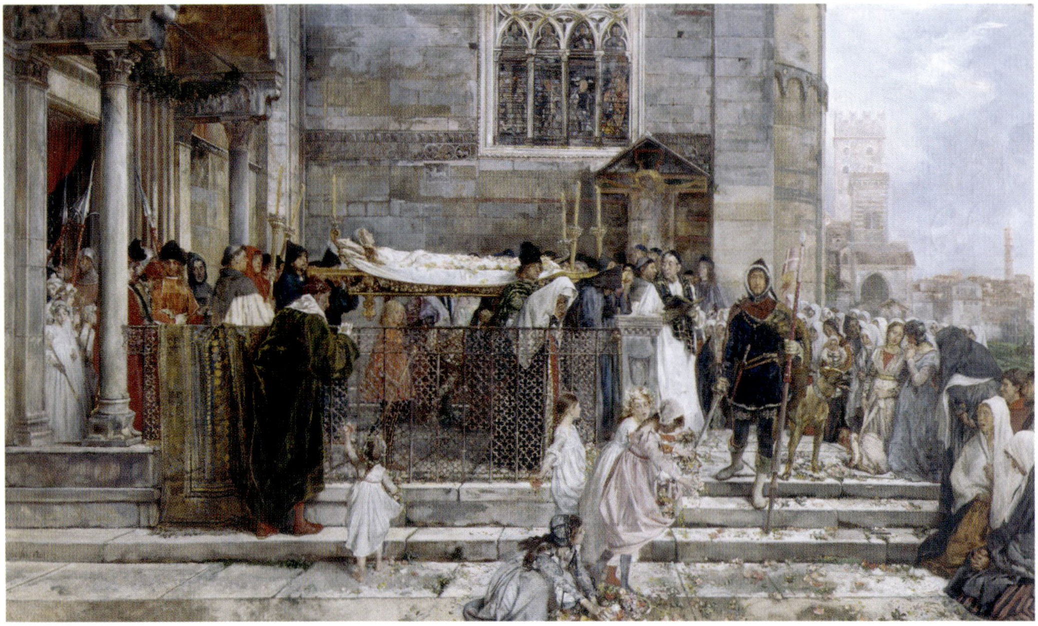

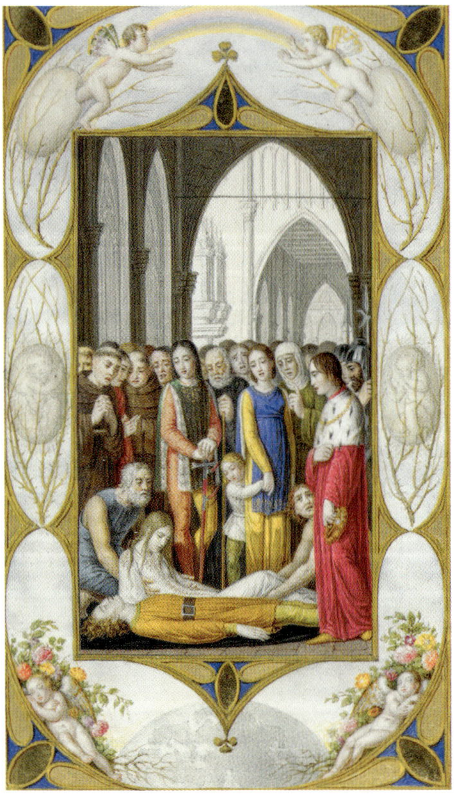

↑ **Scipione Vannutelli**
Juliet's Funeral, 1888, Rome, Galleria Nazionale d'Arte Moderna

↖ **Giambattista Gigola**
The Public Display of the Bodies of Romeo and Juliet, c. 1819, Milan, Biblioteca Trivulziana

which had never previously been depicted: at the centre of the composition, light appears to shine from the ghostly contour of Juliet, as she lies asleep. In *Romeo at Juliet's Deathbed* this tension instead appears to be sublimated through the ecstasy of love. The same tragedy acquires a sumptuous and theatrical air in Frederich Leighton's painting *The Reconciliation of the Montagues and Capulets*, executed in the years 1853-1855 (a sketch and watercolour from this work are preserved in the Yale Centre for British Art). The painting depicts the closing scene of the play, set in the crypt of the Capulets, when the two old patriarchs shake hands as a sign of peace and the Prince – portrayed between the two, at the centre – brings an end to the tragedy with his words. It is fruitless and destructive hatred – the Prince wisely observes – that triggered this senseless drama, defeating even love's most powerful arguments:

> "Capulet! Montague!
> See, what a scourge is laid upon your hate,
> That heaven finds means to kill your joys with love. [...]
> A glooming peace this morning with it brings;
> The sun, for sorrow, will not show his head:
> Go hence, to have more talk of these sad things;
> Some shall be pardon'd, and some punished:
> For never was a story of more woe
> Than this of Juliet and her Romeo."[21]

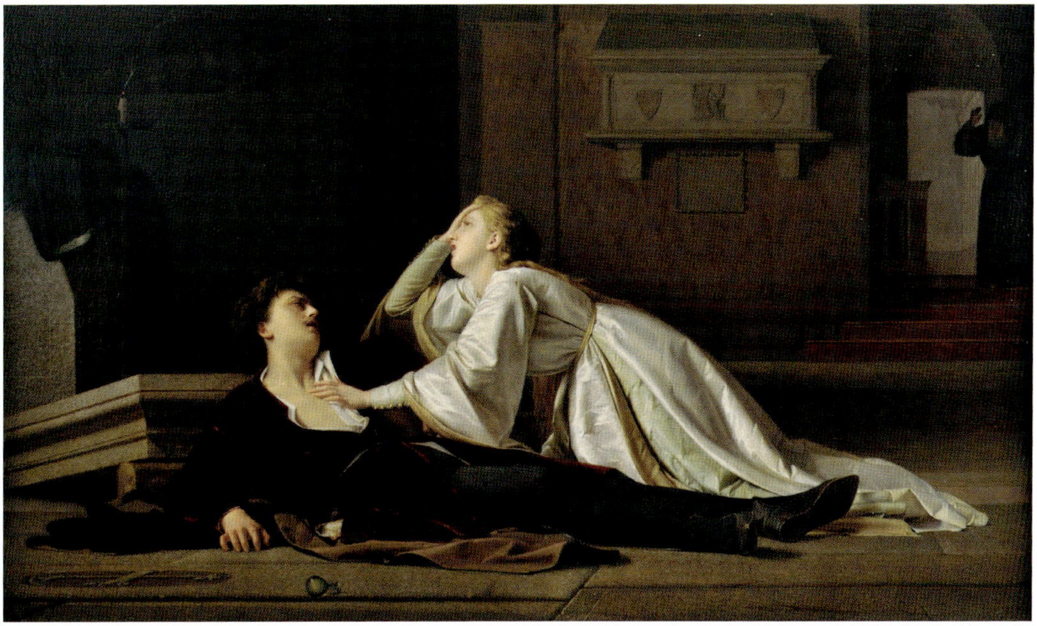

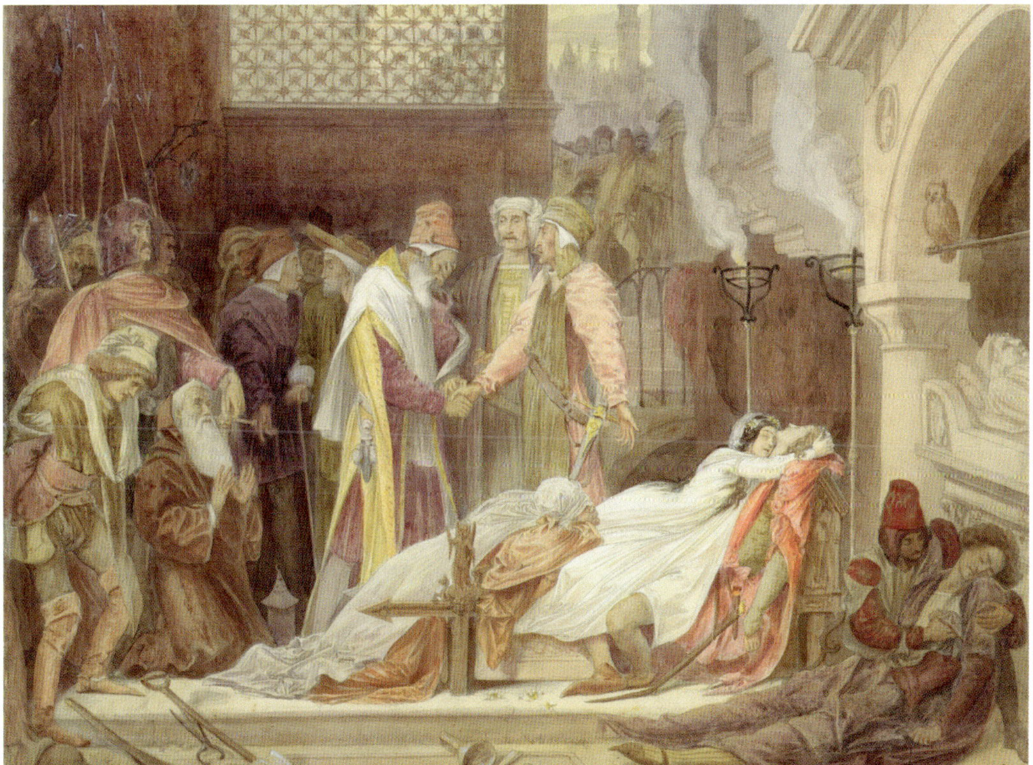

↑ **Pietro Roi**
The Death of Romeo and Juliet, c. 1860, Vicenza, Museo Civico

↑ **Frederich Leighton**
The Reconciliation of the Montagues and Capulets over the Dead Bodies of Romeo and Juliet, 1853-1854, Yale Center for British Art

From Painting to Music and Cinema

Juliet's tale was often put into music in the 19th and 20th century. Among other operas, we might mention *Giulietta e Romeo*, with verses by the prolific Genoese librettist Felice Romani and music by Nicola Vaccaj, which was first staged in Milan in 1825 and in Genoa for the Carnival of 1827. From an adaptation of this work Vincenzo Bellini produced *I Capuleti e i Montecchi*, which was first presented at the Teatro La Fenice in Venice on 11 March 1830 (with the famous mezzo-soprano Giuditta Grisi in the role of Romeo). Charles Gounod lent a more sentimental quality to the story – particularly through the duets between its two protagonists – in his *Roméo et Juliette*, which was first staged at the Théâtre Lyrique in Paris on 27 April 1867. Riccardo Zandonai explored the same theme in his opera *Giulietta e Romeo* (first staged at the Teatro Costanzi in Rome on 14 February 1922), a musical drama with a marked lyrical streak, emphasized by a distinctive use of orchestral colours. Finally, drawing upon the charm of instruments alone are Hector Berlioz's *Romeo et Juliette* of 1839 – a dramatic symphony for a chorus and orchestra – and the ouverture fantasia written by the young Peter Illyich Tchaikovsky in 1869 (and later revised in 1880). In the 20th century the tragic and so visually evocative tale of the two young Veronese lovers could not but find its place on the wide screen – as it continues to do so today.

In 1936, George Cukor directed a sumptuous version of *Romeo and Juliet*, engaging the most prominent theatre actors of the day: Leslie Howard, who was already forty-three at the time, Norma Shearer – a thirty-four year-old Juliet (but one married to a Metro Goldwin tycoon) – and the great John Barrymore, a capricious alcoholic who played a wonderful Mercutio. Among many other transpositions, we might recall the most elegant 1954 film *Romeo and Juliet* by Renato Castellani, starring Laurence Harvey, Flora Robson and Susan Shentall. Particularly unforgettable is the rarefied scene of the ball in the Capulet house. In 1968 Franco Zeffirelli presented a new version of the tragedy, in which the leading roles were played by the very young actors Pat Hetwood, Olivia Hussey, John McEnery, Milo O'Shea, and Leonard Whiting. The film received two Academy Awards (one awarded to Pasquale de

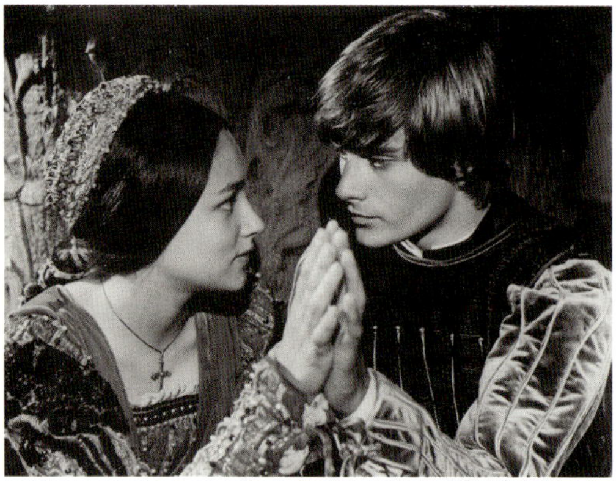

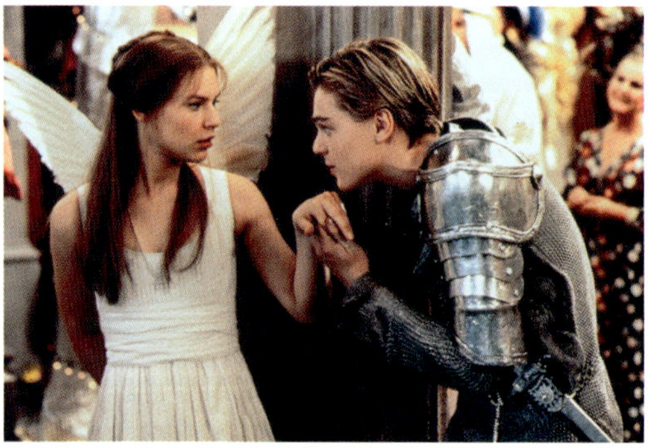

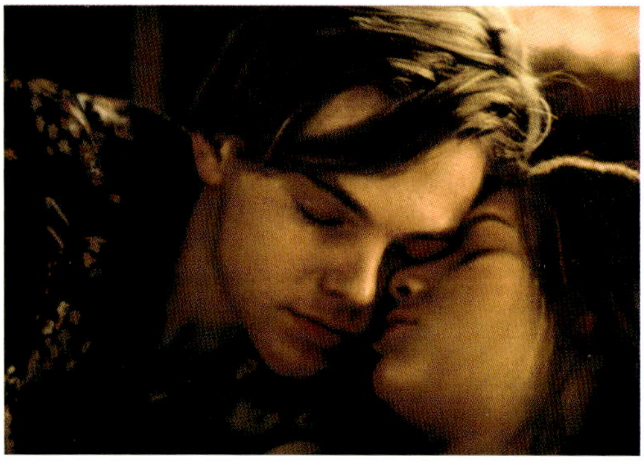

Santis for Best Cinematography, the other to Danilo Donati for Best Costume Designs). Aesthetically refined and charming as only great theatre can be, the film features an amazing soundtrack composed by Nino Rota. What struck people the most at the time of its release was the professional skill of its two protagonists, who were barely fifteen and seventeen years old Baz

→ **Leopold Metlicovitz**
Poster for *Romeo and Juliet*, music by R. Zandonai, libretto by A. Rossato

← **Franco Zeffirelli**
Frame from the film *Romeo and Juliet*, 1968

↙ **Baz Luhrmann**
Frames from the film *Romeo + Juliet*, 1996

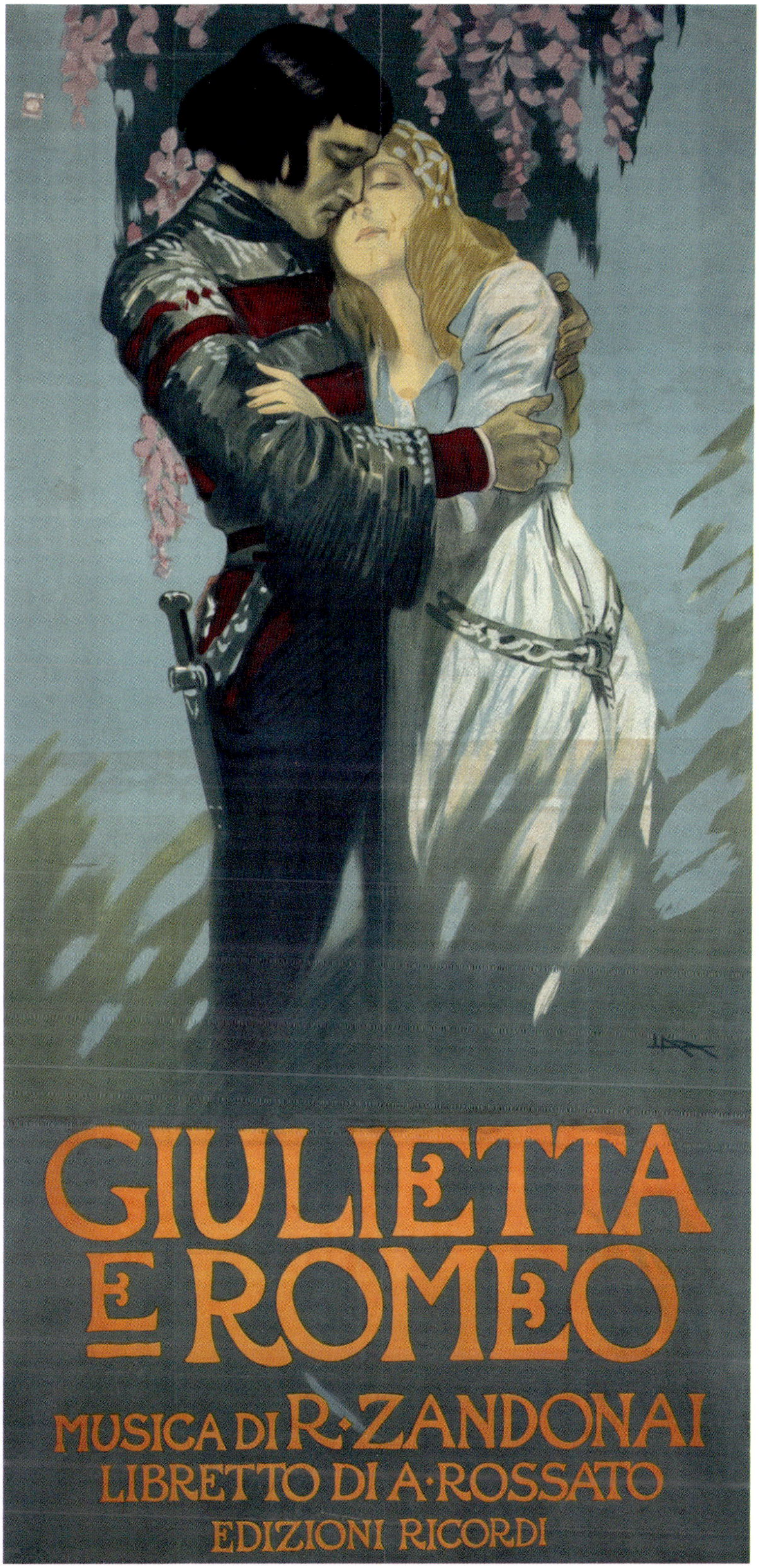

Luhrmann's 1996 film *William Shakespear's Romeo + Juliet* brings out the unique quality of Shakespeare's play, which constantly transposes and blurs the boundaries between truth and falsehood. This somewhat over-the-top, turbulent and irreverent film stars Leonardo DiCaprio and Claire Danes at their début (in 1997 both actors were quite rightly awarded for their performances. Most faithful to the Shakespearian text in its dialogues, it is set in an imaginary suburb of Los Angeles filled with lights and sounds. The partisans of the Montagues and Capulets are turned into gang members cruising in big American cars; the heads of the rival families are presented as tough bosses, and the sharp and moody Mercutio is turned into a Black transvestite (Harold Perrineau). The director's chief aim was probably that of conveying the lifelike quality and moving pathos of an ill-fated, young love.

With all the theatrical, musical and cinematographic transpositions still being made, many are the winding paths along which the "fair tale" continues to unfold today – its memory safeguarded in the House of Juliet. While times and languages may have changed, Juliet remains the genuine and vibrant heroine of the story – a sensitive, daring, passionate and brave heroine caught by Shakespeare, like Leopardi's "light and thoughtful" Silvia, in the enchantment of "girlhood's bounds".

The author would like to give her most affectionate thanks to Fausta Cataldi Villari and Rachele Palladino.

[1] W. Shakespeare, *Romeo And Juliet*, Prologue.
[2] *Romeo and Juliet*, act I, scene I.
[3] *Ibid.*, act I, scene I.
[4] *Ibid.*, act I, scene II.
[5] *Ibid.*, act I, scene V.
[6] *Ibid.*, act I, scene V.
[7] *Ibid.*, act II, scene II.
[8] *Ibid*, act III, scene IV.
[9] *Ibid.*, act V, scene II: "The searchers of the town, / Suspecting that we both were in a house / Where the infectious pestilence did reign, / Seal'd up the doors, and would not let us forth."
[10] *Ibid.*, act V, scene III.
[11] Priamus and Thisbe, two young Babylonians, are in love with each other. As they cannot get married because of the enmity between their parents, they secretly communicate through a crack on the wall separating their houses. One night, they arrange to meet by a spring outside of the city. Thisbe arrives at the appointment first, but flees at the sight of a lioness which has come for a drink, and drops her veil. When Pyramus arrives, he sees Thisbe's veil on the ground, torn and bloodied by the animal; assuming that his beloved has been devoured, he falls on his sword. Thisbe finally makes her way back to the meeting place and in turn commits suicide upon seeing the lifeless body of her lover.
[12] Actually, as Natalino Sapegno observed in his edition of Dante's work, "in the name *Montagues*, Dante sums up – so to speak – the political action begun by the Monticoli family of Verona [...] in *Capulets*, the work of the Guelph forces, as embodied by the Capelletti faction in Cremona."
[13] On this restoration work, see D. Zumiani, 'Giulietta e Verona: spazi e immagine del mito', in *Medioevo ideale e Medioevo reale nella cultura urbana. Antonio Avena e la Verona del primo Novecento*, edited by P. Marini, Verona 2003, pp. 203-221.
[14] *Ibid.*, act III, scene III.
[15] *Ibid.*, act IV, scene III.
[16] *Ibid.*, act V, scene III.
[17] "After I had discussed this matter with Sir Gerardo Boldiero, my uncle, he introduced me to the place and showed me – aside from the aforementioned sepulchre – a niche in the wall towards the portion of the building facing the reverend Capuchin fathers, whence he said that many years ago the grave had been removed, along with some ashes and bones."
[18] Concerning this work, see A. Conforti Calcagni, 'La tomba di Giulietta a San Francesco al Corso', in *Medioevo ideale e Medioevo reale, cit.* pp. 195-201; F. Pesci, *La Verona di Giulietta e Romeo. I luoghi della leggenda shakesperiana*, Milan 1999 (also on the House and its iconographic success).
[19] *Romeo and Juliet*, act III, scene V.
[20] *Ivi*, act I, scene V.
[21] *Romeo and Juliet*, act V, scene III.

Bibliographical Notes

T. Lenotti, *Giulietta e Romeo nella storia, nella leggenda e nell'arte*, Verona 1951.

Romeo e Giulietta dalla novella di Luigi Da Porto. Incisioni di Renzo Sommaruga, Verona 1961.

T. Lenotti, *Palazzi di Verona*, Verona 1964.

F. Dal Forno, *Case e Palazzi di Verona*, Verona 1973.

L. Da Porto, *Giulietta e Romeo*, edited by G.F. Viviani, Verona 1974.

M. Praz, *La letteratura inglese. Dal Medioevo all'Illuminismo*, Milan 1977.

Neoclassico e troubadour nelle miniature di Giambattista Gigola, catalogue of the exhibition (Milan, Museo Poldi Pezzoli; Brescia, Civica Pinacoteca Tosio Martinengo, 1978-1979), edited by F. Mazzocca, Florence 1978.

J.P. Jouvet, *Presentazione*, in F. Butturini, *Di Romeo e Giulietta, di altri e di altro*, Verona 1982, pp. 9-15.

G. Beltramini, *Le strade di Verona entro la cerchia delle mura*, Verona 1983.

Cara Giulietta. Cultura della moda, dell'arte, dell'immagine a Verona, catalogue of the exhibition (Verona, Galleria d'Arte Moderna e Contemporanea, July-September 1984), edited by G. Cortenova, Venice 1984.

G. Bologna, *Giulietta e Romeo nella illustrazione di Giambattista Gigola e nel testo di Luigi Da Porto*, Milan 1985.

Shakespeare a Verona e nel Veneto, Proceedings, edited by A. Lombardo, Verona 1987.

A. Castagnetti, *La signoria scaligera: aspetti politico-istituzionali*, in *Gli Scaligeri 1277-1387*, catalogue of the exhibition (Verona, Museo di Castelvecchio, June-November 1988), edited by G.M. Varanini, Verona 1988, pp. 3-24

N. Cenni, M.F Coppari, *I segni della Verona scaligera*, Verona 1988.

G.M. Varanini, *Signori, società, strumenti del potere*, in *Gli Scaligeri 1277-1387*, catalogue of the exhibition (Verona, Museo di Castelvecchio, June-November 1988), edited by G.M. Varanini, Verona 1988, pp. 111-112.

M.C. Zaniboni, *Un'antica passione. Romeo e Giulietta dalle fonti a Shakespeare*, Imola 1988.

W. Shakespeare, *Romeo e Giulietta*, Milan 2010.

G.M. Varanini, *Istituzioni, Società e politica nel Veneto dal comune alla signoria (secolo XIII-1329)*, in *Il Veneto nel Medioevo. Dai comuni cittadini al predominio scaligero nella Marca*, edited by A. Castagnetti and G.M. Varanini, Verona 1991, pp. 263-422.

D. Zumiani, *Città d'armi, di commercio, di nobili dimore. Inventario ragionato dei Beni artistici, storici e monumentali del comune di Verona*, Verona 1991.

G.P. Marchi, *"Zulieta e Romeo": il piccolo epos contradale di Vittorio Betteloni*, in "Atti e Memorie della Accademia di Agricoltura Scienze e Lettere di Verona", s. VI, vol. XLIII, 1991-1992.

M. Bandello, *Giulietta e Romeo*, edited by D. Perocco, Venice 1993.

A. Grimoldi, *Restauri a Verona: cultura e pubblico 1866-1940*, in *L'architettura a Verona dal periodo napoleonico all'età contemporanea*, edited by P. Brugnoli and A. Sandrini, Verona 1994, pp. 121-193.

G. Guarda, *La lunga storia di Giulietta*, Vicenza 1994.

F. Mazzocca, *Francesco Hayez. Catalogo ragionato*, Milan 1994.

E. Hesselberg, *La vera tomba di Giulietta*, in "Veneto ieri oggi e domani", 73 January 1995, pp. 225-235.

D. Zumiani, *Shakespeare e Verona. Palazzi e cortili della Verona medioevale*, Verona 1996.

Füssli pittore di Shakespeare. Pittura e teatro 1775-1825, catalogue of the exhibition (Mamiano di Traversetolo, Parma, Fondazione Magnani Rocca, September-December 1997), edited by F. Licht, S. Tosini Pizzetti, D.H. Weinglass, Milan 1997.

P. Brownell, F. Curcio, *Verona. Guida storico-artistica*, Caselle di Sommacampagna, Verona 1998.

P. Marini, *Giovanni Battista Cavalcaselle e Verona*, in *Giovanni Battista Cavalcaselle conoscitore e conservatore*, Conference proceedings, edited by A.C. Tommasi, Venice 1998, pp. 165-173.

F. Pesci, *La Verona di Giulietta e Romeo. I luoghi della leggenda shakespeariana*, Milan 1999.

Musei Civici di Vicenza. Dipinti e sculture del XIX secolo, edited by F. Mazzocca, Venice 2000.

C. Parisio, *Giulietta e Romeo nella illustrazione di Giovanni Battista Gigola per Ferdinando III d'Asburgo-Lorena*, Brescia 2002.

A. Conforti Calcagni, *La tomba di Giulietta a San Francesco al Corso*, in *Medioevo ideale e Medioevo reale nella cultura urbana. Antonio Avena e la Verona del primo Novecento*, edited by P. Marini, Verona 2003, pp. 195-201.

M. Guidorizzi, *Giulietta e Romeo da Verona a Hollywood*, in *Medioevo ideale e Medioevo reale nella cultura urbana. Antonio Avena e la Verona del primo Novecento*, edited by P. Marini, Verona 2003, pp. 317-318.

D. Zumiani, *Giulietta e Verona: spazi e immagini del mito*, in *Medioevo ideale e Medioevo reale nella cultura urbana. Antonio Avena e la Verona del primo Novecento*, edited by P. Marini, Verona 2003, pp. 203-221.

M.C. Zoppis, *Verona. La casa di Giulietta*, Rome 2004.

P. Farinotti, *il Farinotti 2009. Dizionario di tutti i film*, Rome 2008.

L. Olivato, *"L'estremo amplesso": la morte di Giulietta e Romeo nella pittura dell'Ottocento; il caso di Pietro Roi*, in *Magna Verona Vale. Studi in onore di Pierpaolo Brugnoli*, edited by A. Brugnoli and G.M. Varanini, Verona 2008.

N. Fusini, *"Di vita si muore". Lo spettacolo delle passioni nel teatro di Shakespeare*, Milan 2010.

T. Tanner, *Preface to Shakespeare*, Cambridge-London 2010.

Baci rubati e amorose passioni, catalogue of the exhibition (Andria, Castel del Monte, 16 July - 1 November 2010), edited by M. Tocci e L. Tonani, Cinisello Balsamo (Milan) 2010.

Photo Credits

Foto Ottica Nodari di Caliaro Nereo: Cover,
pp. 4, 10, 11, 12, 13, 14, 15, 18, 19
Valentina De Lello: p. 19
Matteo Vajenti: pp. 9, 20